# YESTERDAY'S BESTSELLERS

# MORE WILDSIDE CLASSICS

*Please see www.wildsidepress.com for a complete list!*

# YESTERDAY'S BESTSELLERS

## A JOURNEY THROUGH LITERARY HISTORY

by

### BRIAN STABLEFORD

**WILDSIDE PRESS**

YESTERDAY'S BESTSELLERS

This edition published in 2006 by Wildside Press, LLC.
www.wildsidepress.com

# CONTENTS

# INTRODUCTION

This book is the legacy of a youth which almost everyone (myself included, on occasion) would consider misspent. When I should have been out in the wide world, honing my social skills in preparation for the time when I would have to accommodate myself to the society of my fellows, I was in my room reading. There are excuses to be made for such unreasonably eremitic behavior but they do not apply in my case, because I was reading the wrong books. I did read a few of the "right books"—I read so many books that it was difficult to avoid all contact with the great literary minds—but I always preferred the wrong ones. I am reluctant to credit this to bad taste, because I like to think that I am just as sensitive a reader as any other and more sensitive than most, so I am forced instead to attribute it to some mysterious perversity which defies all explanation. Such perversities have their costs, but they also have their benefits; the world would be a truly terrible place if everyone liked the things they were supposed to like.

I discovered most of the writers and books described in these essays entirely by accident, while browsing library shelves or the cheap sections of second-hand bookshops. The exceptions, to which I was somehow guided, I usually reached by unorthodox routes. I went in search of *No Orchids for Miss Blandish* after reading George Orwell's essay, "Raffles and Miss Blandish," because I took it for granted that any book which could arouse such slanderous ire had to be worth reading. When I began buying books from market stalls which allowed them to be traded in for half-price credit after being read, I began to solicit unwanted paperbacks from all my relatives; my dutiful grandmother rooted out a few, but sternly instructed me not to read the Hank Jansons because they were "unsuitable," so I naturally kept the Hank Jansons to read while I swapped the rest for science fiction magazines. There is, however, an especially fond affection which attaches to those books which are the gift of serendipity, and my memories of some of the books discussed herein were assisted in their firm adherence by the sheer unexpectedness of my encounters with them.

I recall reading *Beau Geste* at thirteen and thinking it the best and strangest book I had ever read; it took me many years of grubbing about in second-hand bookshops to assemble a complete set of the author's other works, but I finally managed to locate *Two Feet from Heaven* at the age of forty-three, and read it with a reverent awe which

# Introduction

no one who is not an avid reader can imagine. (I say "avid reader" rather than "book collector" because there is a world of difference between the two; true book collectors never read the books they collect, because the act of reading would endanger the mint condition of the items in question.) P. C. Wren died before I was born and I have every reason to believe that he and I had absolutely nothing in common, but I feel that I have long had an intimate relationship with him; indeed, I am occasionally given to wild flights of fancy in which I suspect that I may be the only person still living who might actually have got halfway to understanding him.

I feel much the same sense of intimacy with most of the other authors considered in these essays—with W. H. Hudson, Robert Hichens, James Hilton, James Hadley Chase, and even poor misfortunate Hank Janson (who suffered in the latter phases of his career from an unusually severe case of split personality, having become a mere "house pseudonym"). The sensation of understanding gained by cultivating a close familiarity with an author's works is probably a delusion, but, if so, it is one worth cherishing and it is certainly one of the most valuable acquisitions of the reading habit. There are doubtless many people who suppose that the kinds of intimacy and understanding one can obtain by reading are less worthwhile than the sorts cultivated by actual acquaintance with living individuals, but that merely supplies proof that everyone is deluded one way or another. Real people are far more distant than works of fiction, and much more prone to lie, although some works of great literature are almost as clever and as scrupulous in their evasions as the common-or-garden liars one would pass every day in the street if ever one went out. Works of popular fiction—whose circles of acquaintance are far wider than those of the most popular people—can be liars too, but they have by definition to be frank, charming, convincing, and easy to get along with.

The kinds of people who despise popular fiction (who are usually the kinds of people most given to snubbing, insulting, humiliating, and generally pissing off their fellow human beings) tend to accuse bestsellers of being unintelligent, formularistic, crude, and unstylish, but this is as unjust as most judgments based in neurotic antipathy. In fact, bestsellers are passably clever, very various, highly individualistic, and peculiarly fascinating. They do need to be approached with a certain sympathy, but so does every other work of art if it is to be sensibly appreciated. It is true that bestsellers are sometimes breathtakingly preposterous in their claims and aspirations, but this merely lends an element of enigma to their enjoyment. I still find it impossible to imagine how anyone could ever have taken Marie Corelli seriously, but that merely adds to the fascination which her works exert upon me, and to the awesome respect which I afford to the wisest of the proverbs spawned by the county of my birth: "There's nowt so queer as folk."

## YESTERDAY'S BESTSELLERS, BY BRIAN STABLEFORD

I wrote most of these essays for an ill-fated magazine called *Million: The Magazine About Popular Fiction*, which perished for lack of support. Its fate was sealed when the biggest chain of bookstores in the British Isles, W. H. Smith's, refused to carry copies on the grounds that there was insufficient demand for such a publication. Given that Smith's is the largest retailer of popular fiction in the land (having secured that position midway through the nineteenth century, in a fashion briefly explained in the essay on *The Last Days of Pompeii*), there is a certain appealing paradox in the notion that they see no demand for a periodical devoted to it, especially when one bears in mind that they carry at least four publications devoted to the aesthetics of military hardware and at least four more about yachting. Such were the tribulations endured by *Million* that the editor stopped paying me for the articles when I was less than halfway through the series, but I loyally carried on supplying them because they represented a fascinating exercise in self-recapitulation and re-examination. I was enthusiastic to discover the roots of the mysterious fascination which these books had held for me, and thus felt driven to complete the exploratory expedition on which I had embarked.

This book is, of course, dedicated to all the other patient eremites out there in the social wilderness whose time is devoted to getting to know writers like Eugène Sue, Edward Bulwer-Lytton, H. Rider Haggard, Robert Graves, P. C. Wren, and all their peers as intimately and as well as anyone nowadays can get to know them—and perhaps as intimately and as well as anyone ever could.

—Brian Stableford
Reading, England
March 1995

# PART ONE

# GETTING AWAY
# FROM IT ALL:

# ODYSSEYS IN EXOTICA

# I.

# THE DESCENDANTS
# OF ROBINSON CRUSOE

*The Life and Strange Adventures of Robinson Crusoe of York, Mariner...Written by Himself*, published in the spring of 1719, was the first ever best-selling novel, and would be a uniquely interesting book in that respect alone. The fact that it has stood the test of time far better than almost all of those which came after it makes it even more interesting.

Crusoe's author, Daniel Defoe, was approximately sixty years of age when he wrote the book, and had been making a living with his pen for nearly twenty years. After failing—sometimes disastrously—in various other businesses, he had become a literary hack of astonishing efficiency; he was so prolific in the variety of his enterprises and signatures that no one really knows how many of the five or six hundred works which have sometimes been tentatively attributed to him he actually wrote. It is possible that no author ever sought popularity more doggedly, or was so ill-rewarded when he achieved it. Had Defoe been paid a royalty on every copy of *Crusoe* that was sold in his lifetime he might have died rich, but the notion of copyright was then in its infancy, and the profits of the book went mainly to the bold entrepreneurs who pirated editions of it as fast as they could print them.

Defoe was a pioneer of many modern literary fields and forms, including soft pornography (*Moll Flanders*), popular pseudoscience (*A System of Magick*), crime reporting (*A General History of the Most Notorious Pirates*), and the drama documentary (*A Journal of the Plague Year*), but Crusoe remains by far his most significant contribution to literary tradition. Anxious to cash in on a success which was enriching so many others instead of him, Defoe turned it into the first volume of the very first trilogy of novels, but its two sequels—which were full of Crusoe's reflections on life, the universe, and everything, but were unfortunately devoid of desert islands—were received with near-total indifference, and have been quite forgotten.

*Crusoe* has now been constantly in print in English for 189 years, and for nearly as long in several other languages. It stands at the head of a whole subgenre of "Robinsonades," which has produced many other bestsellers. The most successful of these include *The Swiss Fam-*

# The Descendants of Robinson Crusoe

*ily Robinson* (1841) by J. R. Wyss Jr. (carrying forward a fantasy privately initiated by Wyss Senior), *The Coral Island* (1858) by R. M. Ballantyne, *The Mysterious Island* (1875) by Jules Verne, *The Blue Lagoon* (1908) by H. de Vere Stacpoole, and *Lord of the Flies* (1954) by William Golding. This line of literary descent presents to the modern reader a sequence of very interesting changes rung upon a single central theme: that of the castaway from civilization forced to build his own microcosmic society from scratch. This motif has remained fascinating to large numbers of readers throughout the entire history of the novel, and thus offers us an interesting opportunity to track certain changing attitudes of popular prose fiction, and to reflect upon the eternal utility of one species of literary fantasy.

\* \* \* \* \* \* \*

*Crusoe* is most familiar nowadays in abridged editions marketed for juvenile readers—the inevitable fate of all "classics" whose subject-matter is more interesting than their stylistic gloss. The book is still studied in universities, but it attracts more attention from sociologists than literary purists because of the analysis of it featured in Ian Watt's book, *The Rise of the Novel* (1957), which presents it as the primary piece of evidence supporting the thesis that the early novel evolved as an embodiment of middle-class mercantile values and attitudes, to flatter and educate a rapidly-expanding audience of middle-class readers. Watt makes much of the fact that even though he is alone on a desert island, with no marketplace in sight, Crusoe's behavior is archetypally that of the capitalist entrepreneur, husbanding his resources, organizing his labor, and making advantageous contracts so as to achieve complete mastery of his environment and make a good living. There is no doubt that Crusoe's experiences do qualify as a exemplary parable of the triumph of self-sufficient individualism, and it is for this reason that he has always been held out as an exemplary hero for the education of young boys—not least by Jean-Jacques Rousseau, who casually asserted in *Émile* (1762) that Crusoe was the one book which could teach a boy everything that could possibly be learned from books.

Most commentators have assumed that *Crusoe* was inspired by the widely-publicized adventure of Alexander Selcraig, or Selkirk, who had been rescued from the island of Más a Tierra by the privateer Woodes Rogers in 1709, having spent more than four years alone there. Some historians, aided by wishful thinking and a single oblique documentary reference, have permitted themselves to be convinced that Defoe actually met and interviewed Selkirk, and that he stole many details of his story from Selkirk's reminiscences. The most striking comparison to be made between the real experiences of Selkirk and the fictitious adventures of Crusoe, however, is how dramatically they differ.

Selkirk, by the time he was found, was in a piteous condition: ragged, diseased, deranged, and almost incapable of speech. It was a near-miracle that he had survived at all. Most men who were marooned—and it was not an uncommon form of capital punishment among the pirates and privateers—perished within days, but Selkirk had two crucial advantages, which made the difference between life and death. Firstly, he had all his possessions with him, including tools and weapons (this was because he had demanded to be abandoned in the course of a quarrel with his captain; the demand was a rhetorical move intended to dramatize the strength of his feeling that his ship was in urgent need of repair, but the captain insisted on taking him at his word). Secondly, the island on which he was abandoned had a flourishing population of goats, which he hunted and husbanded very assiduously for meat and hide.

Even these fortunate circumstances might not have been enough to keep Selkirk alive had they not been supplemented by other slices of luck. He very nearly ran out of black powder before finally contriving to make a fire, and he might easily have been devoured by the island's rats had he not been accompanied by a breeding population of cats. As things turned out, the cats kept the rats at bay while providing the unlucky castaway with a measure of companionship. The marvellous extent of Selkirk's good fortune was, however, trivial by comparison with the gifts of providence which were handed to *Crusoe* by his author. Chief among these were an island far richer in natural resources, a convenient wreck from which enormous wealth could be salvaged, and a pathetically worshipful servant.

Thanks to the generosity of their creator—which Crusoe inevitably takes to be that of his Creator—Crusoe and Friday are able to live in industrious harmony on their island. They are properly grateful for their solitude because they know only too well that the world which surrounds them is swarming with all manner of dangerous evils, including Spaniards, pirates, cannibals, and sharks. Their society in miniature constitutes a perfect microcosm of imperial civilization, even though their beleaguered outpost is a long way out in the wilderness. (The parallel becomes either stronger or weaker than it usually seems when one recalls that Friday was not—as is nowadays commonly supposed—a Negro, but a Carib Indian, and that the actual historical fate of the Carib Indians was to be exterminated by European colonists.)

Subsequent writers of Robinsonades were disposed to be every bit as generous to their heroes as Defoe, if not more so. Wyss does not hesitate to populate his miraculous island with an incredibly rich flora and fauna (extending even to elephants and ostriches), nor does he hesitate to arm his idealized *paterfamilias* with the encyclopedic knowledge required for its expert exploitation. Jules Verne had sufficient naturalistic conscience to balk at such naked extravagance, but over-compensated by borrowing Captain Nemo from *Twenty Thousand Leagues Un-*

13

# The Descendants of Robinson Crusoe

*der the Sea*, and setting him to lurk covertly in the bowels of the island, emerging periodically to bestow anonymous gifts upon the grateful castaways—who are thereby enabled to enjoy far more leisure than their illustrious forebear. If Crusoe's island is a microcosm of the Empire and Wyss's an analogue of the Protestant Family Home, Verne's is surely a conveniently-isolated Gentlemen's Smoking-Room.

All of this is, of course, blatant fantasizing, but that is the whole fascination of the Crusoe hero-myth: it is a heartfelt expansion of the eternally-comforting fantasy of Getting Away from It All. Robinsonades are reassuring and self-congratulatory affirmations of psychological self-sufficiency, and this end legitimates as means any amount of fudging with respect to the question of material self-sufficiency. A Robinsonade is a glorious elaboration of one of the most common daydreams: the daydream which, occasionally but persistently, urges each and every one of us to retire from the nettlesome sting of everyday tribulations to some peaceful haven where one is responsible for nothing save one's own whim, and where one is blissfully free of the burdensome obligations of society. Imaginary relationships which are stress-free and rewarding can, of course, be transported along with the castaway.

\* \* \* \* \* \* \*

It is easy to see, if one tracks the history of best-selling Robinsonades, how our notions of stress-free and rewarding relationships have changed with time, both in terms of the list of relationships which qualify and in terms of the possibility of sustaining them.

Until the end of the nineteenth century, the category of stress-free relationships could readily accommodate mannish or boyish friendship (as in *The Coral Island*), but did not easily extend as far as sexual relationships—although Wyss's castaway parents may be presumed to have enjoyed (if that is the right word) normal marital relations. It is, as many commentators have pointed out, highly significant that Crusoe remains utterly untroubled by the lack of any evident sexual outlet; women are not merely absent from his island, but unmissed. The most significant pre-*Crusoe* story of a society built by castaways was Henry Neville's novelette, *The Isle of Pines* (1668), in which a population of 1,789 people has descended from a party of five, the patriarch George Pine having decided to afford fair and equal treatment to his wife, their two maid-servants, and a young negress; but the Crusoe myth is self-indulgent in a crucially different way. The Edens which Crusoe's descendants regained remained largely free of Eves—let alone Liliths—for nearly two hundred years.

This situation changed very dramatically in the early twentieth century. The best-selling English Robinsonade of the new era was *The Blue Lagoon*, which tracks the adventure of two children, Dick and

Emmeline, cast away on a typically bountiful island. The plot is essentially a long and teasing crescendo building towards the climactic moment when the maturing pair will discover sex. For these two innocents, creator Stacpoole alleges, this will not involve any consumption of the fruit of the tree of knowledge of good and evil; they remain wholly virtuous and unfallen, to such an extent that the idea of their being returned to the world at large becomes repulsive. They are allowed instead to float away in their dinghy, with their babe-in-arms, bearing a cluster of crimson berries whose consumption will guarantee their attainment of painless and permanent oblivion.

Although it was considered to be a daringly naughty book in its time, *The Blue Lagoon* is true to the rich Victorian tradition of stories in which virtuous children are allowed an early and beautiful death so that they may avoid the corruption implicit in joining adult society. It is exceptional only in its suggestion that the moral Fall of Man is not due to sex as such, but to the chains of civilization which surround and pervert it (an argument of which Rousseau would have approved wholeheartedly).

*The Blue Lagoon* was not the first Robinsonade to tackle sexual matters in an allegorical fashion. Its theme was foreshadowed in the more cynically-inclined *The Child of Ocean* (1889) by Ronald Ross (the man who was later knighted for his work on the transmission of malaria), which Stacpoole may well have read (both men acquired their background knowledge by serving as ships' doctors). In *The Child of Ocean* a boy castaway grows to young adulthood as an omnicompetent but uncultured Monster before being re-humanized and civilized by the good offices of a female castaway. The arrival of the girl's searching relatives at the end, however, is a fatal interruption of their love-affair far more brutal than the innocence-saving climax of *The Blue Lagoon*. Another, and somewhat better-known, predecessor of Stacpoole's bestseller was J. M. Barrie's satirical play, *The Admirable Crichton* (1902), in which a party of aristocrats and their servants are forced by circumstance to discard the social roles (including the sex-roles) which shaped their stations in civilized life. As in *The Child of Ocean*, however, Barrie's characters cannot recover their lost innocence, and the possibility of rescue and rehabilitation—half promise and half threat—hangs over them like the sword of Damocles until the thread is finally severed.

*The Admirable Crichton* and *The Blue Lagoon* exhibit a strong sense of the oppressiveness of civilized artifice which is very different from the attitude of all the classic Robinsonades from *Crusoe* to *The Mysterious Island*, in which the castaway's task was always to master, tame, and control the island's wildness. Given the basic allegiance of the Crusoe-myth to the daydream of shedding all burdensome social responsibility, however, these works may be seen as an entirely natural development of the tradition, moving to a more fundamental level of estrangement and simultaneously making an attempt to rehabilitate the libido which is altogether appropriate to a post-Freudian era.

The Rousseauesque glorification of an imaginary state of nature which is so strongly featured in *The Blue Lagoon* is reflected in other near-contemporary works, notably in Edgar Rice Burroughs's ebullient but rather tongue-in-cheek Robinsonade, *The Cave Girl* (1913; reprinted in book form together with a 1917 sequel in 1925), but it was a recklessly sentimental sensibility that was already living on borrowed time. It could hardly be expected to survive the object lesson of World War I, which shattered many illusions about innocence and civilization. The kind of novel which was primarily a vehicle for romance and adventure was by then denied any vestige of respectability, and daydream fantasies were easily decoded and just as easily derided. It is hardly surprising that the best-selling Robinsonade of the middle part of the century turned out to be a brutally cynical account of the reversion to murderous savagery of a party of castaway schoolboys: Golding's *Lord of the Flies*.

\* \* \* \* \* \* \*

Although *Lord of the Flies* aspires to a reasonable naturalism within the framework of its allegory, it does include one astonishing example of authorial generosity; Golding allows his castaways to make fire by using Piggy's spectacles as a burning glass, even though the text makes it quite clear that Piggy is short-sighted, and would therefore have spectacles with concave lenses (which are, of course, incapable of focusing sunlight). The story's message, however, is not in the least undermined by quibbles about the methods which ensure the boys' survival. The real point of the story is flatly and mercilessly to contradict the ultra-romantic view of human nature which had been endorsed in such heartfelt fashion by *The Blue Lagoon*. At the end of the book the essentially decent Ralph, who has been saved from death at the hands his savage companions in the nick of time by the arrival of the Royal Navy, weeps helplessly for the civilized innocence which has been cruelly stripped away from him, and for "the darkness of man's heart."

Actually, Golding's viewpoint is not quite so far removed from Rousseau's as this bleak conclusion makes it seem. His later prehistoric fantasy *The Inheritors* (1955)—a parable in which an Edenic Neanderthal Golden Age is destroyed by the Cro-Magnon ancestors of modern man—endorses the desirability of a hypothetical natural state of goodness while ramming home the lesson that mankind is much further removed from such a state than Rousseau optimistically imagined. In *Lord of the Flies* the reversion to savagery is a victory of superstition and tribal ritual; it is a folly of the craven but socially-formed imagination, rather than the straightforward result of a Darwinian struggle for existence.

16

Golding's second Robinsonade, the less successful *Pincher Martin*, is more obviously ambivalent. Its realism is more ruthless, not only in that Martin is driven mad by his isolation, but also in the final revelation that his experiences have been a momentary hallucination based in the exploration by his tongue of a broken tooth. His resistance to annihilation is heroic nevertheless; what he accomplishes by means of the power of his imagination is a kind of compensation, however inadequate, for the fact that the real world exhibits none of the generosity which Crusoes desire and need so desperately.

As with *The Blue Lagoon*, the plot of *Lord of the Flies* had been strangely foreshadowed by earlier works, most obviously by *Children of the Morning* (1926) by W. L. George. Here, a mixed-sex group of castaway children revert to savagery, but their exile lasts much longer, and their rival tribes—having coped with the traumas associated with the general onset of puberty—pass through their initial warlike phase to achieve stability and contentment. Alas, George argues, such a quasi-Utopian state of being is bound to deteriorate again, because the human craving for excitement is sufficient to reproduce all the violent manifestations of savage behavior whenever life becomes too dull. Thus, George's microcosm has recapitulated, albeit sketchily, the whole great riot of human history before the arrival of the U.S. Navy brings the experiment to an end. The moral offered in the final paragraph argues (as do many speculative novels written between the two World Wars) that history is intrinsically cyclical, and that savagery and civilization are merely different aspects of the same ongoing process.

*Children of the Morning* was presumably an attempt to treat quite seriously an idea which had been used fancifully, for satirical purposes, only two years earlier in Rose Macaulay's *Orphan Island*, in which a group of orphan children are marooned along with the voluntary worker—a clergyman's daughter—who has generously taken their care and education in hand. Under her ultracareful tutelage there eventually emerges an adult society which reproduces in grotesque caricature all the social and religious myths of the English middle-class. When would-be rescuers finally arrive on *Orphan Island*, they find this society stoutly and unconquerably resistant to all their attempts to redeem it from its absurdity. A similarly scathing demolition of the image of a desert island as Eden for a new Adam and a new Eve can be found in Michael Harrison's erotophobic novella, "Transit of Venus" (1936).

What these post-World War I Robinsonades have in common is a scepticism which feels bound to refuse both the celebration of innocence whose most extreme example is *The Blue Lagoon* and the celebration of the process of civilization whose most extreme example is *Crusoe*. It is hardly surprising, therefore, that each of them concludes with some kind of resigned acceptance of certain unfortunate features of the human condition which, although not necessarily inborn, are nevertheless presumed to be ineradicable. Several more recent examples can be added to extend the list, most notably Muriel Spark's mercurially ironic *Robinson* (1958), in which the eponymous hero's idyllic lifestyle fails to survive pollution by new social relationships, and Michel Tournier's bitterly ironic *Friday; or, The Other Island* (1967), in which a benevolent Friday's attempts to teach Crusoe the error of his life-denying imperialist vanities come to naught.

\* \* \* \* \* \* \*

No man, as we are constantly reminded even by people who have never heard of John Donne, is an island. But there are times in all our lives when the idea of being one becomes intensely, if only momentarily, appealing. The burden of conformity—of meeting, or trying to meet the expectations which others have of us; of knowing that our actions are observed by others, accountable to others, judged by others; of cultivating and practising the skills which are necessary to get us by in a complex and confusing world—is so heavy that it is necessary for us to make time for ourselves, and fill at least some of that time with joyous fantasies of escape. We all know, or should, that those fantasies are useful and valuable precisely because they are fantasies, and possess the most vital property of fantasies: the ability to take us away while leaving us exactly where we are, to blot out the reality of our situation while not changing it at all.

(There are, of course, actual escape mechanisms which we employ to release ourselves temporarily from confrontation with our burdensome routines: the annual vacation, the weekend, the evening in front of the telly, the burying of one's head in a book. These form a temporal hierarchy which extends all the way from permanently dropping out to the momentary daydream. In every instance the imagination is allowed a brief triumph over reality; the triumph is brief even for permanent drop-outs, whose dropped-out way of life quickly takes on all the weary routineness of everyday reality.)

The sub-genre of Robinsonades is, by necessity, both an indulgence of this kind of fantasy and a critique of it; every Robinsonade flatters and collaborates with our desire to Get Away from It All, and every Robinsonade reminds us that we can't—not, at least, this side of death (with or without crimson berries). However elaborately we may develop the fantasy of self-sufficiency, and however generous we are in allowing the providential retention of the true necessities of life—whether we think these end with fresh water, food, and fire; or with tools, tobacco, and tea; or extend as far as shelter, servants, and sex-partners—we must in the end consent to be rescued. The best we can hope for is to come back from our sojourn on the desert island with a slightly clearer view of the true nature and possibly dubious merits of the civilization which has reclaimed us. That is why the Crusoe myth, in its original version and all of its echoes, can continue to supply us with beautiful solace on the one hand and ironic food for thought on the other.

As a footnote to this conclusion, it is perhaps interesting to note that the Crusoe myth ultimately swallowed up the real man who probably planted its seed in Daniel Defoe's imagination. Walter Wilson, in *The Life and Times of Defoe* (1830), alleged that Alexander Selkirk was quite unable to readjust to the company of human beings, and went to live in a cave in his parents' garden. There is not an atom of evidence to support this claim (and we know that Selkirk spent two years at sea, in close quarters with Rogers's crew, before he landed again in Britain), but the fact that this deft narrative stroke seems to add a certain aesthetic propriety to the conclusion of a real-life drama is a final testament to the fact that however vital fantasies are to psychological health—and they *are* vital—only madmen can actually live in them full-time.

# II.

## *SHE*

Like many other writers, Henry Rider Haggard had so much difficulty finding a comfortable niche within society that he eventually retired from the fray and sought solace in imaginary worlds far removed from it.  The edging-out process began in childhood when his father, having dutifully sent five of his brothers off to public school (Henry, born in 1856, was the eighth of ten children), decided that he must go instead to Ipswich Grammar School.  He was removed from there, in an equally peremptory fashion, at the age of seventeen.  His father entered him for the Foreign Office examinations, with a view to his joining the staff of Sir Henry Bulwer, who was about to be appointed Lieutenant-Governor of Natal.

How much resentment Haggard felt about being packed off to Africa in this unceremonious fashion is difficult to judge; he was far too much of a gentleman to complain overmuch about it in later life.  There can be little doubt, though, that his estrangement from the stern cosiness of Victorian England became irreparable.  He took another hard knock when the girl he left behind him—to whom he was, as they say, "practically engaged"—decided not to wait for him to return and married another man.

How much inspiration Haggard took from his three-year association with his substitute father-figure Henry Bulwer is also difficult to judge, but he certainly committed himself very firmly to a certain philosophy of enlightened colonialism which was probably Bulwer's.  Nor should we overlook the probable significance of the fact that Bulwer's uncle, who had been forced to support himself by means of his pen for some years before becoming the first Baron Lytton, had been for a while the best-selling of all England's novelists.

After transferring for a while to the staff of Theophilus Shepstone, whose mission was to annex the Transvaal, Haggard suddenly abandoned his diplomatic career in 1879 and bought an ostrich farm.  He went briefly to England, where he acquired a wife—who seems to have patiently endured his deep and long-abiding passion for his first love—but on his return found the Boers in revolt and the ostrich-farming business impossible.  The couple, who now had a baby to look after, quickly returned to England.  Although his wife had expectations—he spent his later years combining his literary career with the administration of the estate which she inherited—Haggard decided to read for the bar. It was in parallel with his studies that he wrote his first books.

\* \* \* \* \* \* \*

Haggard had published a couple of factual articles in 1876-77, but he had caused an absurd but awkward diplomatic incident in the Transvaal by a casual reference to the frequent stoutness of Boer women, and had not been encouraged to risk repeating his error. He was moved to take up his pen again by his anger at the way in which the British government backed down over the Boer rebellion of 1881. He voiced his complaints in a study intended to demonstrate the folly of appeasement entitled *Cetewayo and His White Neighbours*, whose publication in 1881 he had to subsidize. (Cetewayo was the king of the Zulus during their war against the white settlers.)

Haggard next set out to write a novel called *Dawn*. Considering his background and interests, his choice of subject matter was, on the surface, very odd. His purpose was, in his own words, "to produce the picture of a woman perfect in mind and body, and to show her character ripening and growing spiritual, under the pressure of various afflictions." He had some trouble publishing it because the story ended with the death of the heroine—something which the prospective publishers declared to be fatal to the book's chances, and which they made him change.

Haggard reported in a piece which he wrote for *The Idler* in 1893 that a "candid friend" had told him that the book was a failure because the hero was not at all "manly." In the article in question he shrugged off this charge, but one suspects that it wounded him more deeply than he would admit; his later work is very much preoccupied with the notion of "manliness." He added to his off-hand comments the curious but very revealing observation that "With Angela herself I am still in love; only she ought to have died." That single sentence sums up a peculiar fascination with the idea of female perfection which was to haunt Haggard's work throughout his entire career.

\* \* \* \* \* \* \*

Haggard followed *Dawn* with an earnest novel set in Africa, *The Witch's Head* (1884), whose centerpiece was a carefully-researched account of the catastrophic battle of Isandhlwana, at which the incompetence of the British commanders resulted in the slaughter of their troops by the Zulus. The book was moderately successful, but the publishers declined to reprint it in a cheaper edition; Haggard's typically perverse reaction was to conclude that the writing game was not worth the candle, and to give it up. He devoted himself to his legal work, and was called to the bar in 1885.

Haggard soon changed his mind about writing, inspired to do so by the huge commercial success of Robert Louis Stevenson's boys' book *Treasure Island*, which had been published in 1883. His brother Andrew later claimed the credit for his change of mind, saying that he had moved Henry to action by betting him that he could not do what Stevenson had done, but Henry's own account of his reasons was rather more prosaic. Either way, he calculated that he could put his knowledge of Africa to good use in writing a fabulous adventure story of his own, and quickly produced *King Solomon's Mines*. He took far less pains with it than he had with his earlier, "real" novels, and subsequently had to revise some of the more slapdash aspects (it was pointed out to him, for instance, that an eclipse of the sun does not actually last for several hours, as the first edition of 1885 had carelessly alleged).

To label a novel a "boys' book" was not, in the 1880s, to say that it was strictly for juvenile readers; it merely specified that the story would be full of action and adventure, and that it would be very "manly" indeed. Members of the female sex rarely took any significant part in a boys' book, and *King Solomon's Mines* was no exception to this rule; the cackling crone Gagool served only to provide a little local color. The novel glorifies the masculine virtues in no uncertain terms in its portraits of the white hunter and soldier of fortune Allan Quatermain, the aristocratic administrator Henry Curtis, the bluff and courageous colonial officer Captain John Good, and the noble savage Umbopa. These four penetrate the dark heart of Africa to discover a land which not only contains a fabulous treasure-trove of precious stones, but constitutes a kind of earthly paradise, temporarily spoiled because of the displacement of Umbopa (its rightful king) by the brutal Twala.

There is no doubt that Haggard's celebration of manliness in *King Solomon's Mines* was perfectly sincere. Quatermain was to remain one of his favorite characters throughout his forty-year career as a novelist, in spite of the slight inconvenience caused by the fact that he casually killed him off at the end of *Allan Quatermain* (1887). There is no doubt either that the allegory submerged in *King Solomon's Mines*, which celebrates the naturalness of "savagery" against the falseness of civilization, is equally sincere. Its message is that although the paternalistic relationship of white man and black can easily go wrong, to the detriment and degradation of both, there remains the possibility of an ideal kind of association relative to which Victorian England and Zulu tribalism are both corrupt and artificial. The happier aspect of the ending of *Allan Quatermain* puts Curtis in place as the enlightened king of another African "lost race," who has no intention of allowing it to be polluted by missionaries, tourists, firearms, whisky, or any of the other curses which afflicted the outposts of the British Empire.

In spite of all this sincerity, however, it must be remembered that *King Solomon's Mines* was essentially a piece of hackwork, very different in its substance from the matters which Haggard had earlier felt a keen desire to express in fictional form. It is not surprising that when he attempted to follow it up with another boys' book he took off in a new direction, using the same format, but introducing into it a kind of subject-matter which was strikingly original. The story in question not only provided his second bestseller, but became one of the most widely-imitated and parodied books ever written; it was, of course, *She* (1886).

\* \* \* \* \* \* \*

The basic pattern of *She* is similar to that of *King Solomon's Mines*. Like its predecessor, it features an expedition to the unexplored heart of Africa inspired and guided by a mysterious artifact. This time, however, the object of the quest is not a literal treasure-trove but something very different. Leo Vincey is searching for the solution to the unusually vexatious mystery of his own identity, and the key to this puzzle is the immortal, imperious, and murderous Ayesha, alias She-Who-Must-Be-Obeyed.

The objects of Leo's inquiry are supernatural; he is the reincarnation of the Egyptian Kallikrates, who once refused to set side his meek lover Amenartas and claim the immortality offered to him by the charismatic queen, and now he must make that same choice again. He must decide whether to abandon the mundane woman Ustane—who loves him wholeheartedly and has saved his life—in favor of the magical Ayesha. This time around, however, Ayesha attempts to make sure that the choice in question is no choice at all; she disposes of Ustane and then—in a scene whose striking sexual symbolism, produced fourteen years before the publication of Freud's *Interpretation of Dreams*, is presumably unconscious—leads Leo across a narrow bridge above "the very womb of the world" to the place where she hopes their union will finally be consummated. The unsettled and unsettling question of whether what then occurs is or is not a tragedy is fundamental to the book's unique fascination.

Her unexpected annihilation by the climactic eruption of the phallic flame which should have demonstrated her immortality did not end Ayesha's career, any more than death ended Allan Quatermain's. She too was destined to reappear in a number of sequels, including one which brought the two key characters together: *She and Allan* (1921). By the time he wrote that book Haggard had suffered the fate of all burnt-out writers and had descended to ritualistic self-plagiarism, but it was not surprising that he did so. From the time he wrote *She* until his death in 1925 he showed distinct signs of obsessive self-repetition; different versions of the triangular relationship between Leo Vincey,

23

Ayesha, and Ustane recur constantly in his work, afflicting Quatermain in the title novella in *Allan's Wife and Other Tales* (1889), Odysseus in *The World's Desire* (1890), which Haggard wrote in collaboration with Andrew Lang, and many others.

Similar triangles can be found in the work of other Victorian writers, many of whom were fond of forcing their heroes to choose between an assertive, amoral, highly sensual woman and a meek, high-minded, utterly chaste one. The stern pressure of Victorian morality favored the latter, and it was only to be expected that most of the novelists followed suit, but it is not entirely surprising that many of the literary works promoting this moral stance have covert subtexts which yearn—often feverishly and sometimes desperately—for an alternative outcome. Haggard's triangles had much sharper corners than most, and he was one of the very few writers who proposed that the choice was so tough that was no way at all of getting it right. In the first sequel to *She*, *Ayesha* (1905), Leo Vincey gets a second chance to achieve the consummation which prevarication and the cruel hand of fate denied him in the first novel; the consequences of his choice are, however, not one whit less frustrating.

\* \* \* \* \* \* \*

It is worth noting that although Haggard did not manage to publish another book in between *King Solomon's Mines* and *She*, he did write one. *She*, in fact, was dashed off in a mere six weeks after he had spent a much longer and more arduous time painstakingly grinding out a "real novel." *Jess* (1887) contains a bitter account of the Boer rebellion and the capitulation of the British government, and Haggard thought it a much more important work than any mere boys' book, but his publishers and the reading public were distinctly lukewarm in their response. Nevertheless, Haggard was now resolved to make a career of writing. If it were necessary to support his more serious work by writing adventure stories, he was quite prepared to do that.

Haggard never received the recognition for his more serious endeavors that he craved, although he tried with all his might to serve his various ambitions simultaneously by introducing more serious material into his adventure stories and more action into his ambitious novels. He was careful to do appropriate research for his historical novels, for his mock-Icelandic saga *Eric Brighteyes* (1891), and for those of his romances which are set in Egypt and South America, but his hopes of elevating them above the status of his two hastily-written bestsellers were not fulfilled. He wrote a good deal of earnestly propagandist nonfiction, about such topics as estate management, the relationship of Church and State, the Salvation Army, and politics, but he was never taken as seriously as he wanted to be. In the estimation of the world he was, and remains, the man who wrote *King Solomon's Mines* and *She*.

In trying to serve all his ends at once Haggard continued, with dogged obstinacy, to put women rather than men at the center of his work. Many of his books bear their heroines' names or (sometimes more revealingly) their epithets: *Cleopatra* (1889); *Beatrice* (1890); *The World's Desire* (1890); *Nada the Lily* (1892); *Montezuma's Daughter* (1893); *Joan Haste* (1895); *Lysbeth* (1901); *Pearl-Maiden* (1903); *Stella Fregelius* (1904); *Benita* (1906); *Fair Margaret* (1907); *The Lady of Blossholme* (1909); *Morning Star* (1910); *Red Eve* (1911); *Marie* (1912); *The Holy Flower* (1915); *The Virgin of the Sun* (1922); *Wisdom's Daughter* (1923); *Queen of the Dawn* (1925); *Mary of Marion Isle* (1929). As the title boldly asserts, however, it is the central figure of *She* who must be considered the archetype among Haggard's women. (Use of the word "archetype" here is more than usually warranted; the psychologist Carl Jung used Ayesha more than once as a key example of an archetypal image.) If we are to understand Haggard's peculiar fascination with idealized women struggling beneath the oppressive afflictions of circumstance, we must unravel the mystery of *She*.

\* \* \* \* \* \* \*

We may assume, given what he said about *Dawn*, that Haggard created most of his female protagonists with love, or at least with profound fascination. It is, moreover, frequently apparent in the stories—although he usually tempered his judgment with mercy, probably for the same reasons which persuaded him to alter the ending of *Dawn*—that he thought that he ought, in consequence, to kill them off. The fact that he seems to have sincerely believed in the possibility of reincarnation, and in the more elaborate supernatural apparatus which is featured in such occult romances as *Love Eternal* (1918), does not set aside the implicit harshness of this opinion. As in the case of Sir Arthur Conan Doyle, and many others seduced by grief into investing their faith in the fashionable occultism of the day, it was the death of Haggard's son which occasioned his seduction; his faith in reincarnation became intimately connected with his preoccupation with the death of female objects of desire, but was not born of it.

Haggard's attitude to the tragic consequences of sexual attraction is doubly revealing. At the more superficial level, it reflects an awkward double-bind implicit in Victorian morality. The Victorian ideal of womanhood was the chaste virgin who would eventually become an in-house angel offering moral and spiritual support to her husband and children. The problem which some male acceptors of this myth discovered was that actually having sexual intercourse with their loved ones came to seem like a kind of desecration which meant that they could no longer hold them in the highest regard. It seemed even worse if the women in question actually managed to enjoy sex. This view is amply displayed in Victorian fiction at all levels—Dickens was one of its more obvious victims—but is taken to its furthest extremes in the work of popular melodramatists.

This item of Victorian morality might itself be seen, however, as a corollary of a more deep-seated anxiety. The whole point of the plot of *She* is that while Leo Vincey is inexorably drawn to She-Who-Must-Be-Obeyed, he is also intimidated by her. In fact, not to put too fine a point on it, he is terrified by her, not because of her homicidal tendencies—he is, after all, too brave and manly to be frightened by the mere threat of violence—but because of her sexual avidity. Even this would not be particularly disturbing, were it not for the fact that the more frightened he becomes the sexier she becomes; the fact of his intimidation is itself an aphrodisiac.

In the most interesting of the many imitations of *She*, *L'Atlantide* (1919; translated as *The Queen of Atlantis* and *Atlantida*) by the French writer Pierre Benoît, the aphrodisiac effects of intimidation come very close to literal masochism, but no English writer could possibly be so uninhibited, and no English hero could ever entertain the notion of submission to such feelings. The problem which Leo Vincey and other similarly-placed heroes face is that once they have experienced the aphrodisiac effects of their intimidation by someone like She-Who-Must-Be-Obeyed, the opposing female image—Ustane/Amenartas—can never suffice; she can only ever be a moral ideal. No matter how wholeheartedly the hero may approve of someone like Ustane, and no matter how grateful he may feel if she should happen to save his life, he can never find her as sexy as her rival.

This is, of course, a no-win situation for everyone concerned. If the hero is saved from the amorous predator, as Leo is at the end of *She*, he is doomed to feel the loss for the rest of his life, and the reader must infer that he would be unable to accept a substitute even had the available one not been conveniently murdered. If, on the other hand, the hero gives in to the force of his desire, as Leo eventually does in *Ayesha*, he devalues his own manly virtues to such an extent that one infers that he will be unable to live with himself.

In consequence of this, it is no surprise at all that as soon as Leo has made his choice in *Ayesha*, he is, as the text decorously puts it, "slain by the fire of her love"—a metaphor which speaks volumes. There is no way that Leo can have Ayesha; and, by the same token, no way that she can have him. Nor is there any way that Leo, once having caught a glimpse of She-Who-Must-Be-Obeyed, could be happy with a nice girl, or any way that a nice girl could be happy with him.

For those who feel like Leo Vincey—or Allan Quatermain in "Allan's Wife," or Harmachis in *Cleopatra*, or *Eric Brighteyes*, or Odysseus in *The World's Desire*, or Olaf in *The Wanderer's Necklace* (1914)—no happy ending is possible. The only possible ending for a story of this kind is one which releases the characters from the paradox which has trapped them, and the only possible release is death, if not for the woman, then for the man, and sometimes for both. Unfortunately, even death cannot be deemed an honorable release; it is a mere resignation which solves nothing. Thus, at least from the viewpoint of the believer in reincarnation, the majority of these characters are bound to come back time and time again, to try and fail repeatedly, with no hope of any ultimate salvation.

* * * * * * *

Performing this ritual of entrancement followed by execution was by no means the only thing which Rider Haggard did during the course of his long writing career. Some modern critics opine that his best book is *Nada the Lily*, the historical novel in which he chronicled the life and times of Chaka, the greatest ruler and warlord the Zulus ever had, and the man who briefly unified his people into a proto-nation in the early decades of the nineteenth century. Others favor the strangest of his books, which features the strangest of his lost races, *The Ghost Kings* (1908), although it too is a study of a doomed woman. A few like the deeply-felt allegory in which he bitterly attacked the blood sports he had formerly enjoyed, *The Mahatma and the Hare* (1911). The ritual described above was, however, the true heart and soul of his work, and he found the business of writing very tough going when he was trying to do something more cerebral and less personal.

All popular books are parodied and imitated, but the sheer profusion of books imitating *She*—including the parodies which poked fun at it—reveals that it touched a chord in the secret hearts of many other manly men. It stands at the head of a rich tradition of stories of serial reincarnation, which includes Edgar Lee's *Pharaoh's Daughter* (1889), Edwin Lester Arnold's *Phra the Phoenician* (1891), and George Griffith's *Valdar the Oft-Born* (1895). It is also the parent of a school of stories in which Egyptian princesses are miraculously brought back to life, which includes Clive Holland's *An Egyptian Coquette* (1898; revised as *The Spell of Isis*, 1923), Sax Rohmer's *She Who Sleeps* (1928), and John Knittel's *Nile Gold* (1929). It has become the template of the formularistic lost race story as practised by William Le Queux, Abraham Merritt, and E. Charles Vivian. A few of these imitators consented to tack on occasional happy endings in response to what they mistakenly took for the irresistible pressure of popular demand, but most of them knew well enough how inappropriate such endings were.

According to Carl Jung, She-Who-Must-Be-Obeyed is a representation of the anima, an archetype of the collective unconscious which embodies the "feminine side" of a man's nature. As this proposition is quite untestable you can believe that or not, as you please. A simpler view is that many boys' book readers are intimidated by female sexual avidity because they harbor doubts about their ability to match demand

27

with performance, and the manlier their outward pose is, the more they think they have to lose. If such anxieties serve only to amplify sexual desire—as they sometimes do—an unfortunate feedback loop can easily be sealed. Even those boys' book readers who avoid this hazard, by one stratagem or another, are likely to remain aware of it, and are thus able to savor the awful plight of poor Leo Vincey and all his manly breed. If this is the correct interpretation, one can readily understand that a few female readers might get a buzz out of books like *She* too, although they might easily be unimpressed by the manner in which Ayesha's mystique is conveniently blasted apart by that fiery ejaculation which she expected to preserve her passion and power forever.

* * * * * * *

Haggard is still as widely read as most popular authors of his era, but his reputation has suffered along with theirs by virtue of his having espoused views which nowadays seem naïve or politically incorrect. In his own day his attitude to the black peoples of Africa was relatively enlightened, and his racist assumptions were less extreme and far less vicious than those of many of his contemporaries, but they have been superseded nevertheless by modern liberalism. Twentieth-century maps have no space left in which lost races might be located, and the primitive anthropological theories which Haggard understandably took seriously have mostly been consigned to the intellectual dustbin.

Haggard's relatively graceless style provides few grounds for an apologetic case which might lead modern critics to overlook such faults as these. His biographer Morton Cohen in *Rider Haggard: His Life and Works* (1960) carefully guards his own critical reputation by sarcastically lamenting that his subject was more interested in agricultural reform than art. To make matters worse, modern film versions cannot begin to do justice to the range and sumptuousness of Haggard's adventure stories, and the more recent ones play contemptuous havoc with his plots. Victorian morality has become a much-lampooned folly of the past, and modern boys' books—whether or not they accept the guidance of what nowadays passes for consensual morality—do not extol the manly virtues in any fashion much resembling his.

All this does not, however, mean that the boys' book readers and boys' video watchers of today have solved—or even attained palliative release from—the knotty problem to which *She* and much of the rest of Haggard's work is addressed. The modern formula may demand that when all the glamorized designer violence is over the heroine should be saved, and her affair with the hero gloriously consummated, but if one studies the thrust of their plots dispassionately, one can readily identify the same old subtext. Almost without exception, writers of contemporary thrillers seem to feel that their female leads would be safer dead—or at least forever supine.

# III.

# *ALICE IN WONDERLAND*

Lewis Carroll's two books about the dream-adventures of Alice are among the most successful children's books of all time. Like many children's classics, they owe this status to their popularity with adults rather than any uniquely powerful appeal to their intended end-users, but there is no doubt that they do hold and preserve—even nowadays, more than a hundred years after they were written—a fascination which is capable of captivating many young readers. The two books have made a copious contribution to that amorphous common heritage of literary reference which is perfectly familiar even to people who have never read the relevant works. Almost everyone would understand a conversational reference to a Mad Hatter's Tea-Party, or the import of such quotations as "Curiouser and curiouser," "Sentence first—verdict afterwards," and "Jam yesterday and jam tomorrow—but never jam to-day."

The continuing popularity of the Alice books has run in parallel with considerable academic industry, whose bulk and variety far outstrips the academic interest taken in any other children's books. This is mostly due to the nature of the texts; their bizarre incidents readily lend themselves to further exploration and explanation. Martin Gardner's *The Annotated Alice* (1960), which dutifully lays out the original versions of all the rhymes which Carroll parodied, and carefully unfolds the conundrums and verbal tricks which pepper the narratives, is a fascinating extrapolation of the originals. Much additional speculation has, however, been engendered by post-Freudian suspicions about the Reverend Dodgson's relationships with the children he befriended—suspicions which have fed gluttonously on the fact that his keen interest in the emergent craft of photography led him to take many photographs of children, a few of which which were nude studies. Although it is universally accepted that the Reverend Dodgson was entirely innocent of any physical impropriety, the dubious advantage of theoretical hindsight has led many commentators to wonder about secret feelings which he might have had or subconscious desires which he might have sublimated in the writing of the books. Such fantasies have colored the image of the books in spite of the fact that there is little material in the texts which readily lends itself to Freudian decoding.

# Alice in Wonderland

\* \* \* \* \* \* \*

Charles Lutwidge Dodgson was born in 1832 in a Cheshire village where his father was a curate. He was the third of eleven children, but was the eldest son; his two older siblings were both sisters, as were the next two born after him, and it is not entirely surprising that he was always comfortable in the company of young girls. A childhood fever left him deaf in one ear and he had a stammer which stayed with him all his life, at least in adult company, but he was otherwise healthy and evidently came from a remarkably robust family; all ten of his siblings survived him, although he lived to a reasonably good age, dying a fortnight short of his sixty-sixth birthday.

The amazing ingenuity displayed in Dodgson's many and various works was manifest at an early age, not only in making up stories, but also in playing all manner of games and manufacturing various kinds of toys, especially the paraphernalia of conjuring tricks. He was an inveterate tinkerer, always devising new games and modifying the rules of old ones.

Dodgson left Rugby School in 1849 to go up to Christ Church College, Oxford, with which he remained associated in various capacities—most notably as a lecturer in mathematics, between 1855 and 1881—until his death. He was ordained in 1861. After his father's death in 1868 Dodgson moved his sisters to Guildford, and thereafter divided the bulk of his time between Guildford and Oxford. His first book was *A Syllabus of Plane Algebraical Geometry* (1860), and he went on to write several other academic works, including the pioneering text *Symbolic Logic, Part I* (1896), whose intended second part was never completed.

It was in 1856—the year he acquired his first camera—that Dodgson invented "Lewis Carroll" for use on a poem published in *The Train* (the pseudonym was a reversal of a re-Anglicization of a Latin version of his Christian names, Carolus Ludovicus). A month after its publication he first made the acquaintance of the four-year-old Alice Liddell, one of the five daughters of the newly-appointed Dean of Christ Church.

Dodgson was later to declare that the story which grew into *Alice in Wonderland*—one of many whose whose heroine Alice Liddell was appointed to be—was first composed on the "golden afternoon" of 4 July 1862, when he set forth in a rowing-boat with Canon Duckworth, Alice, two of her sisters, and a picnic lunch. Assiduous students of the meteorological records have since assured the world that the weather in Oxford on that particular day was rather poor, but the significance of this particular picked nit is dubious.

Dodgson subsequently presented Alice with a manuscript version of the story he told that day, entitled "Alice's Adventures Under

Ground. " It was not, however, until the novelist Henry Kingsley—brother of the more famous Charles, who published *The Water-Babies* in 1863—saw the manuscript while visiting Dean Liddell that Dodgson was persuaded to think seriously about publishing stories from the remarkable fund he had by then accumulated. Alice's manuscript was subsequently read aloud to the family of Dodgson's friend George MacDonald—who was also to become one of the most important Victorian writers of children's fantasy—in 1863, and MacDonald added his voice to the chorus urging its publication.

Dodgson eventually expanded the 18,000-word "Alice's Adventures Under Ground" into the familiar 53,000-word *Alice in Wonderland*, which was published in 1865. Dodgson was, however, displeased with the typeface of the first edition and had it withdrawn, even though he thought the expense would leave him considerably out of pocket. He need not have worried; following its re-issue in 1866 the book was immediately successful, and in the course of the next thirty years it sold more than eighty thousand copies in the full-priced edition, plus uncounted thousands of cheaper editions.

In the wake of this success Dodgson wrote a sequel, presumably drawing on the same accumulated fund of anecdotes and whimsies, but adding a stronger and more complicated narrative frame by virtue of which the story recapitulates the moves in a rather absurd game of chess. *Through the Looking-Glass* was published just in time for Christmas 1871, but was dated 1872. The text was not quite as Dodgson intended it; the artist who had been commissioned to illustrate both books, John Tenniel, expressed dissatisfaction with one of its chapters, which was omitted. The missing episode was eventually published, more than a century later, as *The Wasp in a Wig* (1977).

Dodgson wrote one more classic work of nonsensical fantasy, the marvellous mock-epic poem *The Hunting of the Snark* (1876), which has many affinities with the Alice books. Unfortunately, he was never able to do anything more in the same vein. The mother-lode which he had mined so avidly had been mysteriously exhausted, and was seemingly incapable of renewal.

\* \* \* \* \* \* \*

*Alice in Wonderland* was a watershed in the history of children's literature whose significance can hardly be overstated. Earlier in the century there had been considerable debate among educationalists as to what was or was not suitable reading for children. Some Utilitarians wondered whether the traditional tales preserved in oral culture for the consumption of children were injurious to a child's sense of reality by virtue of their use of fantastic materials; Charles Dickens was one of several writers moved to protest this idiocy. Almost all of the writers who undertook to produce literary versions of old folk tales—notably

Charles Perrault and the brothers Grimm—took it for granted that part of their task was to turn the tales into moral fables which might play a significant role in the "civilization" of young children, and most writers who took up the task of producing new "fairy tales"—most significantly Hans Christian Andersen—fully accepted a similar duty to moralize. The idea that stories might be written for children which would entertain them without moralizing qualified, in this historical context, an an original and daring one; the idea that calculated nonsense was an appropriate form of entertainment was doubly so.

*Alice in Wonderland* is not without moral sensibility, but the general tenor of its rhetoric is that it is thoroughly sensible and entirely appropriate for children to obtain occasional respite from the demands of duty. Alice is initially put to sleep by a tediously instructive text, and her valiant determination to use the time she spends in free fall productively reciting her lessons is soon put into proper perspective by the time-killing madness of the Mad Hatter's Tea-Party and delightful parodic versions of various popular moralistic rhymes. Isaac Watt's sententiously worthy, "How doth the little busy bee / Improve each shining hour" is neatly transmuted into "How doth the little crocodile / Improve his shining tail."

*Alice in Wonderland* was not the first children's book to make use of nonsense. Edward Lear's *The Book of Nonsense* (1846) had broken the ground, and expanded editions of it had been issued in 1861 and 1863. The most famous Lear poems are, however, of later origin; "The Owl and the Pussycat" and "The Jumblies" first appeared in 1871, "The Dong with the Luminous Nose" and "The Pobble Who Has No Toes" in 1877. Given that most common nursery rhymes had lost whatever sense they might once have had, Lear's earlier innovations cannot have seemed so very striking. Carroll's Alice books went much further even in the realm of nonsense verse, and this was only one of their several aspects. The Carroll books presumably played a key role in assisting Lear to attain the marvellous limits of his own endeavor. 1871 might easily be reckoned the Golden Age of nonsense verse, by virtue of the publication in that year of the two Lear classics and both "Jabberwocky" and "The Walrus and the Carpenter" in *Through the Looking Glass*.

The Alice books are even more striking, however, in the bizarrerie of Alice's encounters with all manner of strange creatures, and in the clever wit which dresses her dialogues with them. Those educationalists who thought it bad for children to be told stories about fairies, either on the grounds that fairies did not exist or because they were creatures of pagan mythology, might easily have felt insulted by the production of a book by a clergyman which not only ignored all matters of piety and plausibility, but which actually took leave to assault and undermine the ethic of self-improvement and the "common sense" of vulgar realism. Although it is conspicuously light at heart,

Lewis Carroll's "nonsense" is never content to be neutral with respect to the "sense" from which it deviates. For the most part it is calculatedly and mercilessly anti-sense. The Alice books are particularly sensitive to those aspects of common sense which only appear to their owner to be sense because they are common and not because they are actually sensible, but their author is conscientious in holding almost nothing sacred.

Perhaps surprisingly, the anarchic quality of Carroll's imaginative work does not reflect any radical sympathies on the part of his alter ego. In real life the Reverend Dodgson was a devout man, a committed supporter of Victorian morality, and so ardent an upholder of theatrical censorship that he thought Thomas Bowdler's version of Shakespeare too liberal. It seems that he considered the Alice books to be a realm utterly apart from the world where the rule of Moral Order was absolute: an innocent imaginary space where—as in Eden before the Fall—such issues were quite irrelevant.

Such observations lend extra significance to the observation that when Dodgson decided, late in life, to write another children's fantasy—one which he intended to be of much higher literary ambition and quality—he undertook the task in a very different spirit. *Sylvie and Bruno* (1889) and *Sylvie and Bruno Concluded* (1893) are certainly not without ingenuity, but they are constructed on a firm moral-allegorical base which so comprehensively wrecks their imaginative ambitions that they seem to be the work of a much less interesting man than the one who wrote the Alice books. The fact that they take aboard some of the mystical and spiritualistic claptrap which came to fascinate Dodgson late in life is also severely to their disadvantage.

Dodgson befriended many other little girls after Alice grew up—when Savile Clarke produced a theatrical version of the stories in 1886 he commenced a long friendship with Isa Bowman, the juvenile actress hired to play the lead—but he never found another Muse. Indeed, it appears that in the absence of her inspiring presence he became sadly suspicious of the merits of the nonsense by means of which he had tried so hard to build a commonwealth of understanding with Alice Liddell.

* * * * * * *

As the title of the second book suggests, the Alice books hold up a mirror to the world of Victorian rationalism, in which everything is comprehensively skewed. The narratives are, of course, dream-fantasies which end, scrupulously enough, with the restoration of all that was disturbed, but at the end of *Through the Looking-Glass* the reader is explicitly instructed to consider very carefully the question of whose dream the tale has been. The Red King has, of course, laid claim to it in the text, and Alice is fully entitled to wonder whether she is the dreamer or the dreamed.

Further to this point, the sentimental poem appended to the second text, which celebrates the meteorologically-unreliable memory of the golden afternoon of the picnic on the river, represents childhood itself as a mental "Wonderland" from whose dream children are unfortunately doomed to wake. It then "consoles" us with a climactic suggestion that the stream of Life down which we are all condemned to drift can also be regarded as a kind of dream.

The historical fate of the Victorian rationalism which the Alice books call so innocently into question is rather ironic. Nineteenth-century positivists thought that they were on the threshold of understanding the universe, and that reason and mathematics were the tools which would enable them to see the authentic sense of things. But when the not-so-slow Mill of Systematic Logic came to grind exceeding small, it revealed to its dutiful but perplexed millers that the fundamental reality of the physical universe was so very peculiar, and so antithetical to common sense, that they were quick to invoke the analogy of Carroll's topsy-turvy wonderlands. In talking about Einstein's theory of relativity, Sir Arthur Eddington, Bertrand Russell, and George Gamow all laid out fairly elaborate arguments based in this comparison; the development of quantum mechanics encouraged further commentaries of the same ilk.

The bewildered Alice, confronting a series of accounts of the world which flatly deny the dictates of common sense, has been transformed by the actual pattern of scientific discovery into a modern Everyman. Natural philosophy's ultimate judgment of the subversive elements of the Alice books is pre-echoed internally by the relativistically-challenged Red Queen, who points out that you have to run twice as hard to get anywhere because you have to run hard just to stay in the same place. "You may call it 'nonsense' if you like," she tells Alice, in her censorious fashion, when told that she is not making sense, "but I've heard nonsense compared with which that would be as sensible as a dictionary."

Nor is it only in the problematic world of modern science that the Alice books have supplied useful metaphors. Numerous political satires have borrowed the method and apparatus of the Alice books, including C. E. M. Joad's *The Adventures of the Young Soldier in Search of the Better World* (1943). More recently, the interest in alternative states of consciousness aroused by the LSD boom of the 1960s put Tenniel's illustration of the hookah-puffing Caterpillar into a new perspective; the sound and image of Jefferson Airplane's Grace Slick singing "Remember / what the Dormouse Said..... / Feed your head! / Feed your head!" became one of the enduring monuments of the decade. All of this would have disappointed the Reverend Dodgson as much as it would have astonished him.

The Reverend Dodgson knew, of course, that many of Alice's encounters touched on authentic philosophical problems. Elementary problems in logic crop up in the conversation of most of the characters in the first volume, while more abstruse questions about the significance of names and the status of general terms are obliquely raised in such sequences in the second volume as that which deals with Tweedledum and Tweedledee and that which features Humpty Dumpty. In drawing out this playful potential, however, the author may well have been as blissfully unaware as young Alice of the extent to which these questions would remain perversely vexed as logic, philosophy, and mathematics continued their convoluted evolution. He must have been fully aware of the fact that his careful recomplication of the notion of dreaming at the end of *Through the Looking Glass* raised issues which had been more ardently and earnestly discussed by religious and rationalist philosophers alike, but had Dodgson found any real cause for anxiety in such questions Lewis Carroll surely would not have indulged them so freely.

To the extent that they are prophetic the Alice books are prophetic by accident, and the Reverend Dodgson might well have been appalled to find them so—every bit as appalled, perhaps, as he would have been by other aspects of modern commentary on the intricacies of the text. Nevertheless, they are prophetic. The optimistic common sense of the Victorians has been comprehensively eroded by modern discovery, modern doubt, and modern cynicism; its rational elements have been shown to be ludicrously simple-minded and its moral elements have been so comprehensively assaulted as to seem to many people to be not merely foolish but actively evil.

Dodgson could not have foreseen such developments in any detail, but he was not without an inkling of the precariousness of Victorian optimism. *The Hunting of the Snark*—in which a Victorian Ship of Fools is steered by reckless heroism, according to the advice of a blank map, to a fatal culminating encounter with the monstrous Boojum—displays a certain ironic and pessimistic awareness. Dodgson's conscientious self-indulgence in the World of Nonsense could not, in the end, exclude a reluctant recognition of the Reality Principle, and it is not entirely surprising that he gave it up thereafter.

\* \* \* \* \* \* \*

It is perhaps unfortunate that the irony of Carroll's all-too-sensible nonsense did not stop with its wry vindication in the worlds of science and politics. The ruthless exposers of the syphilitic worm in the delicate bud of Victorian hypocrisy collected up the Reverend Dodgson with countless others, and set him in the psychoanalytic dock, charging him with secretly—or, at best, subconsciously—harboring pedophilic desires.

Dodgson's apologists have been quick to point out that his interest in taking nude photographs of children was a short-lived whim, and that his doing so was fully sanctioned by the parents of the children involved. They have pointed out that he was also intensely interested, for a while, in taking photographs of eminent Victorian men, and that he gave up the hobby altogether—seemingly without a qualm—as soon as it began to bore him.

The idea that there was any sexual element in Dodgson's interest in Alice Liddell is written off by his apologists as the product of dirty minds unable to conceive of true innocence, and they are very probably right. But even if we are willing to assume—as we surely ought to be—that Dodgson's relationship with Alice was undeserving of any kind of moral or medical stigmatization, we must still recognize that there was something about it which was very precious and uniquely meaningful to him.

Perhaps the significance of his friendship with Alice would have faded easily enough, as it became merely one more in a long series of temporary encounters, had Dodgson not undertaken to prepare the two books for publication, hence conferring unique status upon it. We must remember, though, that he was spontaneously moved to write out the manuscript of "Alice's Adventures Under Ground," and he certainly was not compelled by any kind of commercial or artistic necessity to add the two mawkish poems which serve as preface and postscript to the text of *Through the Looking-Glass*. The second of these says of the Alice of 1862 "Still she haunts me phantomwise, / Alice moving under skies / Never seen by waking eyes," and this sentiment was presumably an honest one.

Save for the mere fact of their existence, the texts of the Alice books offer little insight into the heart of this enigmatic relationship. It is, however, notable that the White Knight—Dodgson's not very flattering parody of himself—is the only individual encountered by Alice in the Looking-Glass world who speaks to her in a kindly and affectionate manner, and who offers her real assistance in an ungrudging manner. Dodgson's alter ego in the first volume is, of course, the Dodo (how many times must the unluckily-afflicted clergyman have stammered over an introduction?), who declares after the caucus race that "Everybody has won and all must have prizes," but instantly appoints Alice as prize-giver and has to improvise a special prize for her when she has unselfishly disposed of all her comfits. There is an intriguing exchange between Alice and Humpty Dumpty when Alice observes that "One can't help getting older"; Humpty Dumpty is inevitably quick to seize the possibility of a misinterpretation, but his reply is more than usually odd. "One can't, perhaps," he observes, "but two can. With proper assistance, you might have left off at seven." Here, surely, there is an authentic depth of feeling, and a message of sorts.

Alice is, of course, absolutely right.  One can't help getting older, and one can't preserve the golden afternoon of childhood, even by the most determined effort.  The carefully-shaped nonsense by means of which the Reverend Dodgson sought to build a bridge into a Heavenly realm which he and Alice could innocently and delightedly share was a perilously fragile structure, and the Wonderland into which it led was not what it appeared to be.  Although it was the most fantastic realm imaginable by one of the most ingenious minds of its era, there was, in the end, far too much maturity in it.

There is no doubt that the Alice books constitute one of the most heroic attempts ever made to get away from the stifling straitjacket of the here and now, but they failed and are all the more interesting because of their failure.  That failure is, in fact, a uniquely marvellous example of the dictum that although truth is certainly stranger than fiction, fiction is—according to its fashion—truer.

The moral of Lewis Carroll's determinedly anti-moralistic books is that it matters not how carefully mad adventurers in the further realms of fantasy may be, nor how resolutely blank are the maps which they carry; in the end, the Boojum is always lurking in place of the Snark, and what we confront at the climax of the nonsensical quest is reality, rudely stripped of all the comforting illusions of familiarity and cant.  Even with "the proper assistance," one can no more "leave off at seven" than all the king's horses and all the king's men could put Humpty Dumpty together again.  Or, as the Dormouse really said (not exactly, but in words much to this effect), only people who live in treacle wells can sensibly refuse to draw anything but treacle.

# IV.

# *GREEN MANSIONS*

The author of *Green Mansions*, William Henry Hudson, was born near Buenos Aires in Argentina in 1841 and lived in various parts of South America until 1869. By that time both his American-born parents were dead, and he came to England, which he regarded as his family's true point of origin. He was by vocation a field naturalist, and most of his published works are essays recording his observations. He was particularly fascinated by bird life, and was co-author of an important work on *Argentine Ornithology* which he and his collaborator compiled in 1888-89. He was later to write a notable book on *British Birds* (1895).

Although he was a scrupulous observer, some of Hudson's work on the wonders of the natural world exhibits a more meditative streak. Various philosophical asides interrupt *Idle Days in Patagonia* (1895) and *Nature in Downland* (1900), but it was not until the work he published in the year of his death, *A Hind in Richmond Park* (1922), that such meditations moved to center stage. The science of ecology had not then been properly demarcated or named—the concept was not popularized until the publication of Charles Elton's *Animal Ecology* (1927)—but if the notion of an ecosystem had been familiar, Hudson would undoubtedly have made use of it in the course of his studies. He had an intense interest in the complex relationships between human cultures and their natural environments, and he was fascinated by such problematic and dubious notions as the balance and harmony of nature. Hindsight allows us to identify him as the most significant pioneer of modern "ecological mysticism," and his two most famous novels are key works in this vein.

In view of the great popularity which ecological mysticism has nowadays achieved—most of its contemporary dogmas being inspired by perverted versions of James Lovelock's "Gaia hypothesis"—it is perhaps surprising that Hudson remains a relatively obscure writer. He was even more unappreciated in his own day. He lived for most of his life in dire poverty; his writing brought in a derisory income, so he and the wife he married in 1876 supported themselves mainly by renting out rooms. This situation lasted until he was sixty, when he was awarded a Civil List pension (on account of his work as a naturalist). Three years later, doubtless belatedly from his point of view, *Green Mansions* (1904) became a bestseller, first in the USA and then in Britain. Only thereafter was he able to lay claim to a modest level of fame.

Hudson's studies of birds were sufficiently well-known by the time he died for Jacob Epstein to be commissioned to produce a commemorative sculpture to adorn the bird sanctuary in Hyde Park. It is entirely appropriate that this work of art—which proved highly controversial when first unveiled on account of its allegedly avant-garde nature—should represent the enigmatic central character of *Green Mansions*: a girl named Rima, who enjoys a supernatural rapport with all things natural, and birds in particular. She is the key symbol of Hudson's distinctive brand of proto-ecological mysticism.

\* \* \* \* \* \* \*

Although Hudson wrote a volume of autobiography, *Far Away and Long Ago* (1918), it takes the form of a lyrical celebration of childhood, and refers to no events later than 1859. His friend Morley Roberts, who wrote a memoir of his later life, did not meet him until 1880, and seems to have learned little about his earlier personal history. Almost nothing is known about the last ten years which Hudson spent in South America; nor, for that matter, is much known about his earliest years in England. He seems to have drifted rather aimlessly about the various emergent nations of South America during the 1860s, and it is quite possible that his first novel, *The Purple Land That England Lost* (1885, known in later editions simply as *The Purple Land*), has some autobiographical elements in it. It is possible, too, that some elements of the early chapters of *Green Mansions* are partly based in experience.

That *The Purple Land* attracted little or no interest on first publication is understandable. It is a rather plotless travelogue, more documentary than novel, describing the romantic misfortunes of its hero following his involvement in the ill-fated revolution of the rebel general Santa Coloma. The story is contained by a gratuitously bleak narrative frame in which it is revealed that the hero spent a long spell in jail after the wanderings he describes so languidly.

In Hudson's later stories of South America a similar bleakness is everpresent, sometimes greatly exaggerated. The novella "El Ombú," the title story of a 1902 collection, is a chronicle of unremitting cruelty and misfortune filtered through the reminiscences of an old man who sits in the shadow of an Ombú tree. "Marta Riquelme"—which Hudson thought the best of his stories—is similarly harrowing; it is based on a legend to the effect that men and women who experience unendurable suffering ultimately undergo metamorphosis into a kind of bird called the Kakué fowl. The luckless Marta is captured by Indians, robbed of her child and so hideously mutilated that when she returns home she is driven away by her own people.

These stories suggest that Hudson was a deeply disillusioned man. Once he emerged from his idyllic childhood and was initiated into the ways of the adult world, his primary reaction seems to have been one of horror. In looking back on those days from a remote distance, he was able to bring an unnatural calmness to his remembrance, but that calmness cannot mask the intense bitterness of his outlook. He was to turn a similarly clinical and cynical eye on life in England in what is thought by some critics to be his finest book, a documentary account of life in a small rural village entitled *A Shepherd's Life* (1910). (This, at least, is sufficiently well-remembered to have been dramatized for TV in the 1970s.)

Between *The Purple Land* and "El Ombú" Hudson wrote two other novels. The later of the two, *Fan: The Story of a Young Girl's Life* (1892 as by Henry Harford), was an attempt to write a conventional three-decker romance, and is pure hackwork; but the earlier, *A Crystal Age* (1887), was a deeply personal book. It was initially issued anonymously, but Hudson readily claimed authorship when it was reprinted in the wake of the success of *Green Mansions*. It is by no means an optimistic book, but it provides the first and fullest development of Hudson's vision of an ideal state of being: an Arcadian earthly paradise in which man and nature live in happy union rather than conflict-ridden opposition.

*******

*A Crystal Age* displays a quasi-religious reverence for the notion of living in harmony with nature, but it carries no political or exhortatory message, and might best be regarded as a fatalist parable lamenting the imperfections of man. The reader is told nothing about the narrator of the story save that he is an Englishman named Smith.

Smith is abruptly and inexplicably projected into a far future when humans live in family communities, each based in a House organized around its Mother. The Mother of the House which takes Smith in is secluded because of illness, and some time passes before he realizes that she is an actual person rather than a symbolic goddess. Although he offends her by not making her acquaintance earlier, she forgives him for his failings and awards him a special place in her affections.

Smith falls in love with a daughter of the House, Yoletta. She appears to be about seventeen years old, but he eventually finds out that she is much older. At this point, the logic of the situation is supposed to become clear to the reader, but it remains beyond Smith's comprehension. Because these people are so very long-lived their reproductive rate must be carefully controlled, and the revered Mother is the only reproductive individual in the House.

Because he cannot grasp this, Smith cannot comprehend why Yoletta fails to understand him when he tries to woo her. Nor can Smith see—although the reader can—that the Mother is grooming Yoletta as her successor, and intends that Smith should fill the role of Father. His failure to understand these matters ultimately costs him dear; while lost in the anguish of his uncertainty he finds a bottle whose label promises a cure for misery, and jumps to the conclusion that it is the means by which his hosts suppress their sexual feelings. He drinks the potion, intending to drown his own passion, and discovers too late what a ridiculous error he has made.

The world of *A Crystal Age* is, in a sense, a reversed image of the world described in "El Ombú"; it is a Heaven formulated to oppose in every way the hellish brutality of the lives of South American peasants. Here, people live in harmony with nature, enjoying the security and stability of the beehive without the loss of individual identity which has made hive society into a horrific stereotype in so many modern accounts of hypothetical societies. In its own way, however, *A Crystal Age* is every bit as misanthropic as the later story, and there is a perverse cruelty in the process by which the protagonist is forced to destroy himself, having failed woefully to be worthy of the wonderful opportunity which fate has offered him. Smith is presented as an Everyman figure, but if he is also an alter ego of the author—and it is difficult to think otherwise, especially when one compares him to Hudson's other protagonists—then one is forced to the conclusion that W. H. Hudson was a man afflicted with an unusually deep and mordant sense of self-dissatisfaction.

There can be little doubt that the Mother in *A Crystal Age* is a figure of some considerable personal significance to Hudson, although exactly what that significance was is now impossible to determine. His last work of fiction—the only one he published after *Green Mansions*, although it may well have been written earlier—was a children's story called *A Little Boy Lost* (1905), whose young protagonist, Martin, runs away from home to follow a mirage and becomes a wanderer. When Martin becomes homesick it is not to his actual parents that he returns (it has been mysteriously implied, in any case, that he was actually fathered by a bird), but to a surrogate mother, the Lady of the Hills. She rescues him from the baleful world, and smothers him with affection, but he eventually leaves her too, lured away by the distant seashore which is beyond the range of her magical powers. There he is picked up by a ship which—seemingly, at any rate—will carry him off to England, the land his parents left before he was born. It is hard to believe that this text is anything but a cryptic allegory of Hudson's own life.

# Green Mansions

*******

*Green Mansions* might be regarded as a synthesis of the oppo-
sites separately embodied in *A Crystal Age* and "El Ombú." Like the
real world, the world of the story is inhabited by civilized men, who
are totally alienated from nature, and savage primitives, who are in
constant conflict with it. Its protagonist, having fled the comforts of
civilization, also flees the degradations of savagery when he finds a tiny
enclave of the tropical rain-forest in which he catches a brief glimpse of
an entirely different way of being.

By the time the narrator of *Green Mansions* tells his tale he has
become a placid and secretive old man called "Mr Abel"—the name recalls that of the first murder victim, a herdsman jealously slain by the
first agriculturalist, whose murderer then became an accursed wanderer—and the events of the story are long past. The old man explains
that he was once Abel Guevez de Argensola, a Venezuelan aristocrat of
European descent, but lost his heritage and was forced to flee his native
land because of his complicity in an abortive coup.

The main narrative describes how the exiled Abel crosses the
Orinoco into Guyana and then turns west towards Parahuari, in a half-
hearted and ultimately fruitless search for gold. His subsequent wanderings eventually take him to an Indian village somewhere in the re-
moter regions of the Orinoco basin, whose inhabitants live in super-
stitious dread of a nearby area of forest. Although the headman of the
village, Runi, is hospitable according to his own lights, Abel despises
the Indians for their brutality and their slyness, and never feels safe
while he shares their life.

Contemptuous of Runi's talk of demons, Abel makes a habit of
visiting the area which the tribesmen fear, finding it peaceful and beautiful. He is intrigued by a curious voice which he sometimes hears
there, which seems part-human and part-avian. Meanwhile, the headman's nephew Kua-Kó gives him lessons in the use of the blowpipe,
seemingly intent on schooling him for some as-yet-unspecified task.

Abel eventually discovers that the demon the Indians fear so
much is an ethereal girl who can communicate with animals and birds
through the medium of a curious "natural language." It becomes obvious that the natives intend him to be her executioner, but his own urgent desire is to befriend her. At first she avoids him, but finally con-
descends to confront him when he attempts to kill a poisonous snake,
because she will not tolerate killing within her domain. She instructs
the snake to let him alone, but she is almost as fascinated by Abel as he
is by her, and he is bitten while her attention is diverted. He falls unconscious, but wakes to find himself in a small hut, tended while he
remains ill by an old man named Nuflo and the girl, Rima.

42

Rima appears very different now; while in the hut she is colorless and devoid of magic. In the forest she wore a spidersilk sheath, but here she is clad in drab cotton. Nuflo claims that she is his granddaughter, but Abel perceives that this is a lie, and that Nuflo is concealing the girl's true origin from her. Rima wants to know everything that Abel can tell her about the world beyond the forest, and is disappointed to learn that there are no other people in the world like her. She becomes very excited, however, when Abel chances to mention a mountainous region named Riolama, which she recognizes as the original version of her own name. Under pressure, Nuflo admits that it was there that he found her.

Abel attempts to live up to Rima's ideals, but his fallibility is constantly exposed. He cannot resist the temptation to share Nuflo's occasional clandestine feasts of meat. When he eventually returns to the Indian village, he finds that Runi's hope that he might slay the demon for them has faded away, and they receive him in an ominously ambivalent manner. They steal his revolver and try to keep him captive, but he escapes and returns to the forest, soon setting forth with Rima and Nuflo for Riolama.

While they are en route Nuflo confesses the whole story of his discovery of Rima's pregnant mother, from which Abel deduces that she must have been the sole survivor of a catastrophe which overwhelmed the remote valley inhabited by her people. This proves to be the case. Rima nearly dies of disappointment when she can find no trace of her homeland between the desolate mountain slopes, but she recovers in due course, and determines to make a new life with Abel. She goes on ahead to prepare her forest Eden for his coming while he lingers in order to nurse the ailing Nuflo—but when Abel finally arrives, intoxicated by the promise of bliss, he finds the Indians hunting in the forest. While the demon was gone they took possession of her realm; when she returned they cornered her in the branches of a huge and solitary tree and set a fire around it to consume her.

Abel, maddened by rage, allies himself with a rival tribe in order to destroy the Indians who killed Rima. Then, giving way to despair, he lives wild for a time in her forest, accompanied by Nuflo's skeleton and an urn containing Rima's ashes. In the end, sick and gripped by hallucinations, he sets off on a phantasmagoric trek through the rain-forest. He ultimately wins his way back to civilization by courtesy of imagined encounters with Rima's ghost, which instill in him the capacity to rebuild some kind of life. He remains convinced, as he tells his tale, that an eventual reunion beyond death might still be possible, provided that he accepts his lot calmly and forgives himself for his failings.

\* \* \* \* \* \* \*

In terms of its basic structure *Green Mansions* is similar to many other tales in which civilized men encounter magical *femmes fatales* but cannot consummate their extraordinary love affairs. Its appeal to readers was probably not dissimilar to the appeal of H. Rider Haggard's *She*, which had been a runaway bestseller seventeen years earlier and had spawned many imitations. Abel is, however, nothing like the heroes of most Haggardian adventure stories; he is certainly no living embodiment of the values of Victorian imperialism and Victorian sexual morality. He may be intellectually and culturally superior to the Indians, but he is their plaything rather than their natural lord, and he makes little distinction between living on the margins of their social world and living on the margins of his own. (Modern ecological mystics, of course, tend to credit the few remaining South American Indians with a far closer intimacy with nature than westerners enjoy, but Hudson—who knew whereof he spoke—considered the life of forest-dwelling savages to be just as much at odds with nature as the life of city-dwellers.)

There is never any question in *Green Mansions* of Abel bringing Rima back to civilization; his one desire is to live with her in that state of harmony with nature which she alone can secure. Rima has very little in common with the vast majority of the *femmes fatales* of popular fiction, in that her appeal is far more maternal than sensual; the reward which she offers tantalizingly to Abel derives from her ability to organize a private paradise which he and she can inhabit in glorious secluded intimacy. Her sexual attractiveness, while not irrelevant, is a secondary issue.

The popularity which *Green Mansions* enjoyed at the time of its publication must have been closely connected with its ability to excite and communicate a curious quasi-nostalgic passion: a yearning for an imaginary Golden Age—or, in Hudson's carefully-modified terminology, a Crystal Age—of love and tranquillity, which somehow seemed to be located in both the personal and the prehistoric past. Like more modern varieties of ecological mysticism, this nostalgic yearning must have traded on the peculiar, and ludicrously false, conviction that our remote ancestors lived much happier lives when they were more intimately bound to the bosom of "Mother Nature." Such convictions presumably share common psychological origins with the impression many adults somehow carry about—in stark defiance of all known fact and all reliable memory—that childhood is essentially a time of innocence and joy. In embodying the myth of Mother Nature's comforting bosom so neatly and so extravagantly, *Green Mansions* became one of the great escapist fantasies of its day.

\* \* \* \* \* \* \*

*Green Mansions* is one of several notable works which offered early twentieth-century readers visions of alternative worlds where the half-satisfactory cushions and comforts of technologically-supported existence were quite unnecessary. It lacks the obsessive tunnel-visioned intensity of such relatively esoteric works as Arthur Machen's *The Hill of Dreams*, which appeared three years later, but it retains an earnest and stylish dignity of a kind which was to be casually discarded from the more self-indulgent escapist fantasies of Edgar Rice Burroughs, who shot to fame and fortune in the following decade. For this reason, Hudson's novel seems a more balanced, more adult, and altogether more serious work than many others of a similar stripe. Though no less false in its promises, it appears to be more responsible to the reality principle by virtue of the way in which it ruthlessly trashes its ideal. It might be argued, however, that this determined negativity is simply one more species of self-indulgence: a kind of maudlin self-pity.

Like many other ultra-romantic fantasies written by male authors, *Green Mansions* leads inexorably to an embittered admission that all dreams of this general kind are, after all, impossible. Rima dies—as do the heroines of Alexandre Dumas *fils*'s *The Lady of the Camellias*, H. Rider Haggard's *She*, and Robert Nathan's *Portrait of Jennie*, to name but a few—and the fact of her death becomes a curious *rite de passage* which the hero must undergo in order to attain a proper state of enlightened maturity. (Film-makers, who mostly live in mortal dread of downbeat endings, either fail to understand this aspect of masculine romantic fantasy or fear that it might alienate too many female viewers, so the ending of Mel Ferrer's disappointing 1959 film version of *Green Mansions* starring Anthony Perkins and Audrey Hepburn contrives a conventional cop-out.)

Perhaps the ending of *Green Mansions* is, in some respects, preferable to the conclusion of *A Crystal Age*, which might seem to an unsympathetic reader to be closer to black comedy than to authentic tragedy. Abel has a success of sorts, in that he is guided by the kindly spirit of Rima's memory to an acceptance of his own innate imperfections, and those of life in general. This is, in its fashion, perfectly reasonable. Given that the dream is incapable of fulfillment, what other hope can there be for its dreamers?

On the other hand, there is a sense in which Abel's patient acceptance of his lot and his conscientious self-forgiveness do not quite ring true. W. H. Hudson never took advantage of Smith's shortcut to passion's terminus, and lived to the ripe old age of eighty-one, but it is not clear to the careful reader of his works that he ever found the kind of peace which Abel allegedly did. The ability of *Green Mansions* to stir and trouble the emotions of its readers does not depend in any way on the palliative gesture of Abel's self-reconciliation; it is in spite of this ending rather than because of it that the novel carries a strong sense of the true value of the kind of fantasy which it constitutes. The real heart of the story is the feeling it conveys that the power of the imagination to create such images is a triumph of mind over matter, even though the real world stubbornly refuses to deliver up anything to match such wild and reckless hopes.

*Green Mansions* is an archetypal example of masculine romantic fantasy, and thus helps to provide an illuminating illustration of one of the most interesting distinctions between masculine romantic fantasy and feminine romantic fantasy. Love stories written by women tend, by and large, to cling determinedly to the desperate hope that happy endings might be possible; love stories written by men mostly accept at an axiomatic level that there is no such animal as a flesh-and-blood woman who is truly worthy to be loved.

It is interesting to wonder why this is, but it remains debatable whether either of these points of view has any connection whatsoever with the world of everyday experience.

# V.

# *LOST HORIZON*

The author of *Lost Horizon*, James Hilton, was born in 1900 in the Lancashire town of Leigh. He was the son of a schoolmaster. His own school days were spent at the Leys School in Cambridge, after which he attended Christ's College Cambridge. While still an undergraduate he wrote his first novel, *Catherine Herself* (1920), and never seems to have seriously contemplated any career outside the literary world. For the next decade he scraped a living writing book reviews for various periodicals for a few pounds a week. He published four more books—one of them, a potboiler called *Murder at School*, issued under the pseudonym Glen Trevor—without any conspicuous success, commercial or critical. In 1933, however, he published the two works which were to make him famous and rich. While the *British Weekly* was serializing his sentimental novel about a schoolmaster, *Goodbye, Mr. Chips* (reprinted in book form in 1934), Macmillan published *Lost Horizon*.

*Lost Horizon* is one of the rare books which have added a new concept to the English language. Shangri-La, the Tibetan lamasery situated above a preternaturally fertile mountain-rimmed valley, in which the heart of the narrative is set, has come to be used with reference to any remote and idyllic retreat from the hostile and confusing world; it has become a modern equivalent of such ancient imaginary lands as Tir-na-noc or the Isles of the Blest. The novel contributed much to the heavily-romanticized notion of Tibet and its Buddhist inhabitants which many Westerners have.

*Lost Horizon* was in many ways a remarkably timely work, in that it offered a delicious escapist glimpse of a haven in which the ominous troubles of the Great Depression and the rise of Fascism in Europe were utterly irrelevant, but it also tapped a deeper and more enduring vein of feeling which connected it to some of our oldest and most cherished myths. The book went through three editions between September and December 1933 and three more in 1934. It won the Hawthornden Prize, and went on to become the basis of one of the most celebrated Hollywood films of the '30s, directed by Frank Capra. The success of Capra's film opened the way for Hilton to move to Hollywood himself, where he enjoyed spectacular but unfortunately short-lived success.

# Lost Horizon

The film version of *Lost Horizon*, starring Ronald Colman, was made in 1937. In the same year a film version of one of Hilton's earlier novels, *Knight Without Armour*, was made in Britain with Robert Donat and Marlene Dietrich. *Goodbye, Mr. Chips* was adapted as a radio play before it too was filmed in Britain—again starring Donat, with Greer Garson—in 1939. Hilton initially went to Hollywood to work as a scenarist on the adaptation of his next novel, *We Are Not Alone* (1939), but he remained there during the war years. He worked with several other writers on the scenario of the classic morale-booster *Mrs. Miniver* (1942), and adapted his own *Random Harvest* (book 1941; film 1942) for the screen. *Mrs. Miniver* won that year's Academy Award as best picture, while Hilton received the Award for best screenplay for *Random Harvest*. Although it was directed by Cecil B. DeMille and starred Gary Cooper, his next morale-booster, *The Story of Dr. Wassell* (1944), was disappointing, and his subsequent work made little impact. He remained in California after the war, and died in Long Beach in 1954.

\* \* \* \* \* \* \*

The central story of *Lost Horizon* is enclosed by a frame narrative in which a man named Rutherford tells the notional author about his puzzling encounter with Hugh Conway, an official in the British consular service who went missing after a rebellion in the Indian city of Baskul forced a disorderly evacuation. Rutherford explains that he found Conway in a mission hospital in a remote region of China, suffering from amnesia; he tried to bring the man home, taking an eastbound ship from Shanghai, but Conway recovered his memory en route when he found himself playing a certain piano piece. At the earliest possible opportunity Conway turned around and set out for the Far East, but had time enough beforehand to explain to Rutherford what had happened to him after leaving Baskul. Rutherford explains that he found it difficult to accept the story, at least in the beginning, because of certain implausibilities—including Conway's assertion that he learned the piano piece which triggered his recovery from a musician who had studied under Frédéric Chopin (Chopin died in 1849).

In the story which Rutherford then relays, Conway escapes from Baskul in a light aircraft in the company of three others: his assistant, Charles Mallinson; an American businessman named Henry D. Barnard (whose real name, it later transpires, is Chalmers Bryant); and a missionary named Roberta Brinklow. Some time after take-off they realize that their uncommunicative and inaccessible pilot is a stranger and that they are headed in an unexpected direction: towards the Eastern ranges of the Himalayas.

Eventually, the airplane crashes in the higher reaches of the Kuen-lun mountains, in a hostile snowbound wilderness, and the mysterious pilot is killed. Conway and his companions are found by a group of Tibetan hillmen who come to them carrying a palanquin which bears an ancient and inscrutable individual named Chang. The evasive Chang—who seems to be expecting them—takes them to the lamasery of Shangri-La, which presides over a fertile valley in the shadow of a curiously symmetrical mountain called Karakal ("Blue Moon"). Although the valley is all but cut off from the outside world, its inhabitants have managed to import a few luxuries from the world beyond, including books, musical instruments, and modern plumbing.

At first Conway and his companions see no one but Chang and a Chinese girl named Lo-Tsen, who plays the piano for them. Conway, who has been somewhat overstressed by his involvement in desperate diplomatic attempts to preserve the disintegrating British Empire, is glad of the chance to rest and browse in the lamasery's large but rather eccentrically-stocked library. Mallinson, on the other hand, is anxious to get away, and becomes impatiently fretful when he is told that he must stay for at least a month, until the porters who bring in goods from the outer world next visit the valley.

In time, the other two members of the party decide that they might as well remain where they are. The missionary decides that God must have guided her to Shangri-La in order to convert the people of the valley, although they hardly seem in need of redemption, given that their life is free of all stress and strife. Bryant, who is a wanted man, decides that there is no point in risking the wrath of the law. Their decisions are, however, of little relevance; their presence in Shangri-La is accidental. It was Conway, and Conway alone, that the pilot was sent to hijack, and it is he that the secretive High Lama of Shangri-La wishes to recruit to his cause.

\* \* \* \* \* \* \*

The focal point of the text is the dilemma which faces Conway and the state of mind which forms the context of his choice. In the novel—less so in the film, not because its script distorts the book (the changes made to the cast of minor characters are irrelevant), but because of the intrinsic limitations of cinematic discourse—Conway is the only real character, and the real labor of the narrative is the precise delineation of his private predicament.

Conway has built a reputation for courage by virtue of his exploits in the consular service, but his imperturbability under pressure is not really born of bravery; it is instead a curious kind of spiritual anesthesia which has possessed him ever since the Great War. The reader is never told exactly what Conway's wartime experiences were, but is left in no doubt that they have affected him very deeply. The world has come to seem meaningless to him, and he perceives himself as one who stands apart from the mainstream of human history, incapable of any true moral commitment. Despite the relentless efficiency of his diplomatic endeavors, his heart has never been in his work; for fifteen years he has felt spiritually lost. When forces beyond his control take command of his life he surrenders to their authority with relief, if not wholehearted gratitude.

Eventually, Conway is let into Shangri-La's secrets. The High Lama turns out to be a European named Father Perrault—perhaps, although the text makes no such suggestion, some distant relation to the famous French poet who set out to convert folktales into fairy tales so that they might be used as a cunning educative device for the "civilization" of young children. Perrault has lived for centuries, having discovered that the valley holds the secret of longevity. He has dedicated his long life to building a safe haven where the heritage of human knowledge may be preserved—a haven which he believes to be vitally necessary, for it is obvious to him that the world is heading for a new and even more destructive war, and for a catastrophic collapse into bloody barbarism. Conway is the man he has chosen to carry forward his work; his is the mind for whose solace and revivification the pocket-Utopia has been carefully designed and fitted.

The worm in the bud of this beautiful relationship is the appropriately-named Mallinson, who construes Conway's inertia as a pernicious moral failure. Mallinson is a coward at heart, and dares not attempt the dangerous climbs which he must undertake in order to reach the outside world without Conway to lend him strength. When the porters finally arrive, Mallinson tries desperately to persuade Conway that all the High Lama's promises are lies, and offers the "proof" that Lo-Tsen is willing to go with them, although the High Lama has told Conway that she is very much older than she seems and would age very rapidly indeed were she ever to leave the valley. Conway's recently-rekindled faith and hope are still very fragile, and are easily subverted; he simply dares not believe in the perfection of his dream, and he agrees to go with Mallinson.

What happens afterwards is well-known, even to many people who have never actually seen the film or read the book. In the film, of course, the transformation-scene is quite explicit; it is a previously-unparalleled dramatic high-point which has since been so frequently imitated that no modern viewer can possibly appreciate the effect it had on contemporary cinema-goers. In the book, however, the situation is much less clear. It is the very last line of Rutherford's narrative which reveals that when Conway was found in Chung-Kiang he was in the company of a Chinese woman, reported by the local doctor as having been the "most old of anyone I have ever seen"; but this cannot be conclusive evidence of the truth of Conway's story, not least because it leaves conspicuously unsolved the enigma of why, if Lo-Tsen really was more than eighty years old, she was prepared to leave the valley.

The point of this ambiguous ending is not to leave the reader wondering whether Conway's story might have been an elaborate delusion; it is more subtle than that. Conway, at the critical point in the plot, does not dare to believe in the reality of Shangri-La, but he finds the requisite courage once he finds himself back in the dark and troubled outer world, not because he now has adequate proof, but because he now has adequate strength of mind. The thrust of the ending (recapitulated, to the best of his ability, by Capra in the film) is to provide a challenge to the reader, requiring that Shangri-La be accepted on the strength of faith and hope, even in the absence of crucial material proof.

\* \* \* \* \* \* \*

There can be little doubt that *Lost Horizon* was a deeply personal book—every bit as intimately personal, in its own way, as *Goodbye, Mr. Chips*. In various directories Hilton listed his recreations as music and mountain-climbing, and it is noticeable that music and mountains play crucially significant roles in both books. That curious nostalgia which informs so many Englishmen that their schooldays were the happiest days of their lives, which saturates *Goodbye, Mr. Chips*, is by no means absent from *Lost Horizon*; when Conway is asked whether there is anything in the outer world remotely like Shangri-La, he confesses that it reminds him, just a little, of Oxford (a comment considered sufficiently noteworthy to warrant preservation in the pages of the *Penguin Dictionary of Quotations*!)

In spite of their considerable differences at the surface level, Hilton's two most famous books have the same story buried within them, defining their structure and their emotional force. It is the story of a heartsick man who miraculously finds his heart's desire in a most unexpected place while far from home, and then proceeds to lose it again. The schoolmaster who loses his wife to unkind death has no means of literal recovery—even one as potentially hard-won as the one which leads Conway to jump ship—but he does have the legacy of a personal transformation, which carries him forward regardless and grants him a kind of salvation.

It is worth noting that *Random Harvest*, which is the story of another amnesiac hero, this time returned from the wars, who must learn to love his devoted wife all over again, is in essence the same story in yet another setting. Like the earlier books, *Random Harvest* is very moving, but the only other work in which Hilton managed to generate any real strength of feeling was *We Are Not Alone*, which embeds a similar threat to emotional security in a more conventional melodrama of murder and betrayal.

James Hilton left no account of his personal history sufficiently substantial to allow his readers any real insight into the more intimate meanings which these themes had for him. This absence of particular detail matters less than it might, though, because the spiritual state which is attributed to Hugh Conway—however idiosyncratic it may seem at first glance—was closely akin to that of many men who had lived through the Great War.

The war which we now call World War I left an indelible scar on the minds of many British writers of the period. Whether they had actually fought in the trenches, or served in some non-combatant capacity on the battlefields of northern France, or simply suffered the tribulations and deprivations of life in wartime England, many Britons felt that a terrible lesson had been offered to them that they must learn or perish. Implicit in this lesson was an apocalyptic vision of an all-too-probable future: a vision of civilization teetering on the brink of annihilation by fleets of bombers which would one day rain high explosives, incendiary devices, and poison gases upon towns and cities, factories, and homes. The scientific romances of the period between the wars are full of anxious fantasies of this kind. Edward Shanks's *People of the Ruins* (1920), Cicely Hamilton's *Theodore Savage* (1922), Miles's *The Gas War of 1940* (1931; reprinted as *Valiant Clay* under the author's more familiar pseudonym, Neil Bell), John Gloag's *To-morrow's Yesterday* (1932), H. G. Wells's *The Shape of Things to Come* (1933), and S. Fowler Wright's *Prelude in Prague* (1935) are among the most notable examples. *Lost Horizon*, on the other hand, stands virtually alone as a daring, desperate, and—in the end—fatally-compromised antidote to these same anxieties.

It was easy enough for people who had lived through the Great War, and thought themselves sensitive enough to have understood what a foul and wretched war it had been, to believe wholeheartedly in Hugh Conway's spiritual anesthesia, and to sympathize, at least to some degree, with his relief in the temporary abandonment of all moral commitment. It was easy enough for such people to accept that the call of duty which was poured like poison into his ear by the cowardly Mallinson was a treacherous temptation, and to wish as fervently as they could that he might hear the voice of true sanity and turn back, forsaking the evil world for the lovely dream. As the Great Depression tightened its grip on Europe and America alike, it was easy enough to think that the world was doomed, and to feel, in self-consciously perverse fashion, that it so thoroughly deserved its doom that an honestly cynical man might just as well look forward to seeing it go to hell. To that state of mind, intoxicating news of a safe haven where the world-weary might surrender their souls to eternal bliss could be very welcome, even if it were mere illusion.

* * * * * * *

52

It is not altogether surprising, given all this, that *Lost Horizon* appealed equally to prize-giving critics and ordinary readers, nor that it caught the imagination of the tireless engineers of the Hollywood Dream Factory. It is, admittedly, an eccentric novel, but it is certainly no more eccentric than other notable British novels written in the same year which encapsulate other aspects of the same *zeitgeist*. In H. G. Wells's future history *The Shape of Things to Come*, only a quasi-Fascist Air Dictatorship can save the war-ravaged world for Socialism. In Osbert Sitwell's *Miracle on Sinai*, guests in a luxury hotel on the eponymous mountain discuss the sad state of the world, fall out over the proper interpretation of new Tablets of the Law delivered by a glowing cloud, and watch helplessly as a cataclysmic new war begins. In John Cowper Powys's titanic *A Glastonbury Romance*, small miracles abound in a convoluted plot which is part Grail-Quest, part exorcism of sadistic impulses, and part-Manichean fantasy, leading up to a climax which takes the form of a rhapsodic hymn to the Earth-Mother Cybele.

*Lost Horizon*'s critical reputation has not survived into the present. It has never been promoted to the university syllabus, nor is the book much read nowadays by aficionados of popular fiction. The film continues to please audiences in cinemas and on TV—especially in the reconstructed prints which have recovered the greater part of Capra's own version (which was insensitively pruned after its initial release because the studio bosses thought it intimidatingly long at two full hours)—but there are special reasons for its continued success; Ronald Colman's performance as Conway is excellent—as is his performance as the amnesiac soldier in *Random Harvest*—and it is a triumphant central work in the canon of one of the great Hollywood directors. The film will doubtless continue to be exhibited as one of the classic products of its period even if the book is completely forgotten, and it is of course the film rather than the book which inspired Leslie Halliwell's reverent but somewhat lackluster sequel, *Return to Shangri-La* (1987). It would be a pity, however, if the book were to be completely eclipsed by the film, because it is only in the pages of the original text that the true nature and depth of Conway's feelings is revealed and explored, and it is only in the pages of the text that the true timelessness—as well as the timeliness—of those feelings can be properly appreciated.

Today's world is, perhaps surprisingly and perhaps depressingly, uncannily similar to the world of 1933. The 1990s have, at any rate, more in common with the 1930s than any intervening period has had. The Second World War proved, after all, not to be the apocalyptic affair that so many people feared, and it paved the way for a long period of sustained economic growth. The atom bomb was a more-than-adequate replacement for poison gas as the great bugbear of future war stories, but the fearsome apocalyptic anxieties it engendered were themselves cause for hope that the ultimate tragedy could be averted—that the contemplation of nuclear holocaust would prove a deterrent to any sane warmonger. Now, though, we have become prey to other apocalyptic anxieties which arise from the manner in which we are despoiling and destroying the Earth's ecosphere, and it is easy to believe that the situation is already well out of hand, beyond anyone's power to halt. The specter of Depression has returned, too, to haunt the rich nations as well as the poor. In such a time, the emotional force of the central myth of *Lost Horizon* may once again become all too easy to feel.

In the six decades which separate us from the time when James Hilton was pouring out his heart upon the pages of *Lost Horizon*, the notion of an actual Utopia—even such a tiny, fugitive Utopia as Shangri-La—has become distinctly unfashionable. The modern pattern of hopeful escapism looks neither to a better place (eutopia), nor to a better time (euchronia), but rather to a better state of mind (eupsychia). Even desperate dreams have withdrawn from the arenas of the world, the nation, and the neighborhood, and the hopes we pinned to the home are dwindling in their turn. We are clinging now to the last straw of all: the conviction that although the only peace and satisfaction we can really attain is a private peace of mind, we might just be able to manage that if only we could somehow sort ourselves out. The modern Shangri-La, or Sangréal, is buried deep in our own hearts.

This does not mean, however, that visions of a place of rest, and of a community blessed with harmony, have become redundant. However we may redesign our hopes, we are not alone, and we must at least be prepared to import vital supplies from the outer world if life is to be worth living. Unless we can look outwards to horizons which are not yet lost—even if they exist only in the imagination—there to find images which embody and exhibit our ideals, how will we recognize peace of mind if and when we find it?

# PART TWO

## HOW DIFFERENT IT SEEMS NOW:

## THE PAST AND OTHER FOREIGN COUNTRIES

# VI.

# *THE LAST DAYS OF POMPEII*

The great tradition of nineteenth-century English literature mostly consists of very long novels. This is not because the writers of the period were naturally long-winded—indeed, the labor of producing 250,000-word books with the inefficient pens of the day must have been a sore burden to many of them—but because of price-fixing in the book trade.

Until the end of the Napoleonic wars book production was relatively expensive, and the standard price was ten shillings and sixpence per volume. In order to make books more easily available to those who had the leisure to read, circulating libraries sprang up. These institutions allowed their members to borrow one volume at a time, exchanging it as often as they liked, for an annual subscription of one shilling. The proprietor of the largest circulating library, Charles Mudie, had a strong vested interest in retaining, at least for the most sought-after items in his stock, a high purchase price and a multi-volume format. Because he took such a large proportion of the print run of new novels, he was able to dictate terms to the publishers, who steadfastly maintained both the price and the format of novels until the last decade of the century, in spite of all the advances in technology which made production much cheaper.

Because of Mudie's market-rigging, there was a wide gulf separating the world of upmarket publishers from those which served the demands of poorer readers as literacy gradually spread to the lower classes. The latter produced cheap magazines and serial parts for a penny a time, and their compactly-packed products, which were inevitably aimed at the lowest common denominator of popular taste, became known as "penny dreadfuls." Although a few prestigious novelists—most notably Charles Dickens—were anxious to reach the emergent audience, it was not easy to bridge the gulf which Mudie and the upmarket publishers were enthusiastic to maintain. Some publishers of cheap reading material were keen to publish the works of famous writers, but the copyright holders could see little profit in allowing works to be produced in such cheap formats when more comfortable profit margins were available elsewhere.

This situation began to change in the 1850s, largely because of the rapid expansion of the railway network. Victorian train journeys were long and uncomfortable, and station bookstalls were well-placed to do a roaring trade in inexpensive books. The leading operator of station bookstalls was the firm of W. H. Smith, the legacy of whose success is still obvious today, and several publishers began issuing series of "railway novels"—frequently known as yellowbacks because of their brightly-colored cheap cardboard bindings—in order to supply Smith's bookstalls with cheap and portable reading-matter.

The railway travellers were, of course, predominantly middle class, and many would not have wanted to be seen reading vulgar penny dreadfuls, even if their eyes had been up to the task of reading such microscopic print on a swaying train. The publishers of railway novels therefore looked around for respectable novels which could be reissued in the new format. As chance would have it, the novelist and statesman Sir Edward Bulwer-Lytton had just bought back the copyrights on his early novels, which the publisher considered to be "worn out," and he sold them *en bloc* to Routledge, the leading publisher of railway novels.

Thanks to this accident of timing, Bulwer-Lytton became the most popular of all best-selling authors, proclaimed as such mainly on the basis of the copies sold by W. H. Smith's myriad stalls. Although the prolific writer of historical romances G. P. R. James had far more titles available (forty-seven as opposed to nineteen), it was Bulwer-Lytton who became the outstanding success of the new medium, and the best-selling novel of the mid-nineteenth century railway boom was *The Last Days of Pompeii*.

* * * * * * *

Bulwer-Lytton had been born Edward Bulwer in 1803. His father was a general and his mother was the heiress of Knebworth in Hertfordshire. He was educated by a series of private tutors and published his first volume of poems at seventeen, at which age he also fell hopelessly in love. Alas, the girl died, and he later opined that this unhappy experience had marked him for life. At Cambridge he was a star of the Union, but only scraped a pass degree. After a couple of aimless years he contracted a marriage in 1827 which his mother considered unsuitable, and she cut off her financial support, forcing him to make a living with his pen. He became a prolific writer of novels, plays, tales, and sketches. His first novel, the anonymously-issued and steadfastly gloomy *Falkland* (1827), was a failure, but he had learned an important lesson, and it was quickly followed by the light and frothy *Pelham* (1828). Pelham clearly owed its inspiration to Disraeli's recently-successful *Vivian Grey* (1826), although the eponymous dandy is obviously based on the unhappy Beau Brummell (who had long fallen from grace, although his opinions had eventually prevailed in determining the fashion which gentlemen's clothing would follow for the next century and a half).

At the beginning of his career as a writer, Bulwer was a relatively unashamed hack who clung to what literary pretensions he could while churning out work as fast as he was able. His works frequently fell short of the wordage required to fill three volumes, but he padded them out with verses reeled off by the yard and—when he could get away with it—with footnotes. After his first disaster he clung steadfastly to subject-matter which seemed likely to have wide appeal. He followed up his first success with other novels of high society, including *Devereux* (1829) and *Godolphin* (1833). *Paul Clifford* (1830) and *Eugene Aram* (1832) are crime stories which hover uneasily between the scrupulously moral and the calculatedly lurid, the former featuring a highwayman and the second a murderer.

Bulwer was more adventurous in his shorter works, many of which were written for the *New Monthly Magazine* while he was its editor in the early 1830s. These pieces exhibit a fondness for heavy-handed satire and tortured allegory, both of which were combined in his pastiche of Le Sage's *Devil on Two Sticks*, *Asmodeus at Large* (1833). He was, however, fully conscious of the fact that the most popular writer of the day was Walter Scott, and it was inevitable that he should try his hand at the historical novel; *The Last Days of Pompeii* (1834) was the first of his many ventures in this form. Three plays which he wrote between 1838 and 1840 were very successful, and his occult thriller *Zanoni* (1842) became a great inspiration to those lifestyle fantasists who thought it would be a super wheeze to pose as Rosicrucian magi. Most contemporary critics despised him throughout this period, partly because of his popularity, although he was befriended by Dickens and Disraeli, and the widowed Mary Shelley—who naturally sympathized with his defiance of parental authority in the name of love—expressed the opinion that he had the potential to become a great writer.

Having been forced to the margins of his social class by his mother's disapproval, Bulwer temporarily accepted the role of *enfant terrible*. In 1831 he entered Parliament as a Reformer, and although he returned the following year as a Liberal he retained his radical sympathies, openly professing Republican views which were anathema to the mass of the Victorian aristocracy. He was given a baronetcy by Lord Melbourne's government in 1838, to reward his services as a pamphleteer. He had separated from his wife by that time, but was never entirely reconciled with his mother; when he inherited Knebworth from her in 1843, however, he began to revert to type. It was at this point in time that he began calling himself Bulwer-Lytton, the second surname being hers. It was not until he re-entered Parliament as a Tory in 1852, however, that he was once again able to follow in the footsteps of Disraeli, briefly serving in Lord Derby's government before being elevated to the peerage as Baron Lytton of Knebworth in 1866. He died in

1873, leaving his final historical novel, *Pausanias the Spartan*, unfinished.

*  *  *  *  *  *  *

*The Last Days of Pompeii* is in many ways a typical example of Bulwer's literary method. Having decided to aim at Scott's audience, he determined to outdo his model in the scrupulousness of his research, the vividness of his plot, and the relevance of his morality (historical fiction was, of course, intended to be educative in more ways than one). Statesmen of the day were always fond of drawing analogies between the burgeoning British Empire and the glorious Roman Empire of old, despite the fact that the Roman Empire had been coupled for all time, by courtesy of Edward Gibbon, with the ideas of Decline and Fall. Literary works about decline and fall were, in any case, in vogue; there had been a recent rash of catastrophist fantasies, including three entitled *The Last Man*: Thomas Campbell's poem (1823), Thomas Hood's parody, and Mary Shelley's novel (1826), all of which rejoiced in the delicious sadness of contemplating the end of everything. (Philippe Aries's classic study of attitudes to death, *The Hour of Our Death*, calls this period in history "The Age of Beautiful Deaths," on account of the fashionability of making much of the rectitude and propriety of ostentatious mourning.) Bulwer could see the melodramatic potential of setting a novel in the shadow of a pressurized volcano, and he knew that the intellectual climate would lend him a certain seriousness with which to dignify the melodrama.

The ruins of the two cities which had been buried by the eruption of Vesuvius in A.D. 79 had first been discovered in the late sixteenth century by tunnellers attempting to excavate a water-channel, but serious excavation did not begin until 1709. The finds made then in Herculaneum sparked off a long series of treasure-hunts. Pompeii itself remained virtually untouched until 1748, and it was not until 1763 that an inscription was discovered which confirmed that the site was indeed Pompeii. By 1834, however, the discovery of the ash-entombed city had been widely popularized; these were the early days of popular tourism, and the extensive press coverage given to the rather haphazard excavations put a heavy stress on the romance of antiquity and the educative value of the prizes plundered from the ground. (Disciplined archaeological excavation of the site did not begin until 1860.) The moment was exactly right for Bulwer to exploit his subject to the full.

It is perhaps a pity that Bulwer could hardly wait to cash in on his brilliant idea, and rushed the book through; it is the most obviously padded-out of all his novels, and yet is remarkably clipped and abrupt in the final chapters, which describe the eruption and the fates of the various characters. What should have been an extraordinarily spectacular climax turns out in the event to be almost dull. The power of the theme proved, however, more than adequate to compensate for Bulwer's faltering execution. Today, when dozens of Hollywood movies have reduced climactic volcanic eruptions to the status of mere *cliché*, and hundreds of polished thrillers have honed the craftsmanship of melodrama to near-perfection, it is not easy for readers to see what the audiences of the 1830s and the 1850s saw in *The Last Days of Pompeii*; there is, however, a sense in which it remains a stubbornly interesting book, fascinating in its idiosyncrasies if not its primary intentions.

\* \* \* \* \* \* \*

The plot of *The Last Days of Pompeii* is a curious concatenation of melodramatic *clichés*. The handsome and cultured Athenian Glaucus falls in love with the beautiful Ione. Unfortunately, Ione's brother Apaecides has recently become a priest of the Egyptian goddess Isis, whose cult is enjoying considerable fashionability in Pompeii because of the "miraculous" pronouncements made by the stone image in here temple. Apaecides is the *protégé* of the high priest Arbaces, who secretly admires Ione and is determined to have her for his own. Ione does not suspect this, because the priests of Isis are supposedly ascetic and celibate. Their pose is, however, merely a front—like their faked miracles—and in the privacy of their temple their inner circle holds secret orgies. When the authentically ascetic Apaecides is initiated into this inner circle he is sorely distressed, and becomes attracted instead to the popularly-despised asceticism of Christianity.

One of the many slaves hired from their owners to play a part in Arbaces's orgies is a blind girl named Nydia, who is bought by Glaucus to save her from ill-treatment at the hands of the aforesaid owners. She falls deeply in love with him, and her unhappiness at being made a go-between in his pursuit of Ione is further compounded when Julia—the daughter of a rich merchant—recruits her as a go-between in her doting pursuit of the unsuspecting hero.

The cunning Arbaces tries to poison Ione's mind against Glaucus, but his success is temporary and he is revealed in his true colors. He and Glaucus fight and Apaecides helps Glaucus, much to Arbaces's annoyance. Arbaces discovers that Julia intends to try to seduce Glaucus by means of an aphrodisiac potion obtained from an old witch who lives in a cave on the slopes of Vesuvius, and he tries to persuade the witch to supply her with a poison. The witch will not go that far for fear of reprisal, but agrees instead to supply a drug which will make Glaucus mad. Julia's plan is thwarted by Nydia, who exchanges a phial of water for what she believes to be the love-potion, but is subsequently tempted to use the potion on her own behalf. While Glaucus is wandering around, maddened by the drug, Arbaces murders Apaecides to prevent him revealing the fraudulent nature of the temple miracles and then says that he saw Glaucus commit the crime. Glaucus is condemned to be executed in the arena, sent forth unarmed to face a lion.

Nydia finds out the truth, but is imprisoned by Arbaces. Another priest has also witnessed the crime, but his attempt to blackmail Arbaces goes awry and he too is imprisoned. Nydia manages to send a message to one of Glaucus's friends, the Epicurean Sallust, but Sallust is too drunk to read it until the time for the execution is due. Fortunately, the preceding gladiatorial contests—described in a tone seemingly borrowed from the contemporary coverage of boxing matches by Pierce Egan—over-run, and Glaucus is saved from the lion in the nick of time, just as Vesuvius begins to erupt. Glaucus has then to race through the fire-deluged streets to save Ione from the clutches of Arbaces, accomplishing this with an ease which testifies to the author's impatience to be done with his plot. While the Christians run hither and yon through the hail of fire—exultantly proclaiming that "The Hour is Come!," Glaucus and Ione are separated, but the loyal Nydia brings them together again. Having thus redeemed herself for her earlier follies, Nydia secretly throws herself over the side of the ship which bears them to safely.

\* \* \* \* \* \* \*

In one highly significant respect, *The Last Days of Pompeii* had to walk an ideological tightrope. Even the earliest of Scott's romances had been set within the secure moral bounds of Medieval Christendom, whose ideas of virtue and vice could be taken for granted, but the Pax Romana in A.D. 79 was a world whose moral life was based on assumptions very different from those embodied by that unparalleled paragon of Christian virtue, Queen Victoria (who was, of course, fervently admired by everyone except Republicans). Earlier British dramatists, including Shakespeare, had written about ancient history without difficulty, but that which can safely be left offstage in a play is more difficult to leave out of account in a novel, and the exploits of Thomas Bowdler—who died five years before Victoria ascended the throne—demonstrate the extent to which attitudes had changed since Shakespeare's day. Bowdler's other famous victim, Edward Gibbon, had ruffled a few feathers thirty years before by representing the conversion of the Roman Empire to Christianity as a phase of its decline rather than a kind of salvation, and Bulwer was undoubtedly aware of this controversy and its after-effects.

Bulwer must have been tempted to pander to the piety of his mass audience by making the destruction of Pompeii the act of an angry but just God, wreaking vengeance upon the pagans for their persecution of the early Christians, but his Radical conscience simultaneously pulled him in the opposite direction. For this reason, the role played in the novel by the Christian faith is an oddly ambivalent one. Although

Arbaces is the villain of the piece, and is duly destroyed in the climax, there is little rejoicing in his fate to compensate for the elaborately lyrical account of his world-view which had been given a few chapters earlier. Bulwer was presumably aware of Blake's comment, which was to be further elaborated in Shelley's *Defence of Poetry* (written in 1821, but unpublished until 1840), that Milton had been "of the Devil's party without knowing it," and he might well have been conscious of the fact that in spite of the sops which his novel carefully offers to Christian expectations, he had given all the best lines and all the most interesting thoughts to Arbaces.

Although Arbaces's pose as a priest of Isis is hypocritical, it is clear that his true faith—a sceptical philosophy which substitutes the "Necessity of Nature" for the gods but includes a secret wisdom inherited from Egypt—is one with which Bulwer has much sympathy. Arbaces, who has an alias which links him with Hermes Trismegistus, one of the legendary forefathers of the occult tradition, is one of a whole series of Bulwerian mystics, which had begun with the enigmatic Volktman in *Godolphin* (1833), and was to continue with the modern magi who are the central characters of *Zanoni* (1842) and *A Strange Story* (1861). None of these characters is a hero, but all of them are infinitely more charismatic than the effete individuals who become their victims, pupils, or enemies.

Bulwer always remained sceptical about the occult, but it continued to fascinate him, and he was equally sceptical (although he was careful never to say so too loudly) about orthodox religion and Victorian morality. When Glaucus announces his conversion to Christianity in a postscript to *The Last Days of Pompeii*, even a devout reader might have been tempted to think that it is an entirely suitable fate for such a preciously high-minded prig.

\* \* \* \* \* \* \*

All this is perhaps more interesting because it has to remain submerged. Victorian puritanism ruthlessly repressed the fascination which English writers might otherwise have found in contemplation of the exotic glory of pagan antiquity. Things were, of course, very different in France, where Montesquieu had preceded Gibbon in offering his *Considérations sur les causes de la grandeur des Romaines et de leur décadence* (1734); many subsequent French writers became fascinated by the decadence of Rome, with all that the word might imply. Bulwer's description of the orgies which allegedly took place in the secret precincts of the temple of Isis is inevitably anemic, with no explicit reference to sexual intercourse, but French writers were not so coy. The most famous French depiction of life in ancient Pompeii is that contained in Théophile Gautier's visionary fantasy "Arria Marcella" (1852), in which a tourist slips back through time to enjoy a luxurious

love-affair with the eponymous courtesan.  Gautier's hero is eventually
returned to the modern era by the curse of Arria Marcella's spoilsport
father, an enthusiastic Christian convert, but he considers this a cruel
banishment to a state of eternal misery.

Bulwer's real interests and sympathies were forced to remain
submerged in his art and in his life, and the same is true of many of
those who came after him.  The occultist Madame Blavatsky borrowed
extensively from his works, including *The Last Days of Pompeii*, but
attached her supposed esoteric wisdom to a distinctively Victorian
morality; and the most successful writer of the English *fin de siècle*,
Marie Corelli, produced similarly sanitized visions of antiquity in novels like *Ardath* (1889).  Gautier's successors in France, by contrast,
produced dozens of novels in which the world of Classical Antiquity
becomes an exotic paradise of sensuality, and the majority were enthusiastic to side with the Epicureans against the callous denials of Christianity.  The best-known examples in English translation are Gustave
Flaubert's *Salammbô* (1863), Anatole France's *Thaïs* (1890), and Pierre
Louÿs's *Aphrodite* (1896), but many of the more lushly ornate—including Jean Lombard's *L'Agonie* (1888) and *Byzance* (1890)—have
never been translated.  In France, that which Bulwer could not seriously
contemplate became quite practicable.  Alphonse Louis Constant, who
posed as the magus and custodian of secret wisdom Eliphas Lévi, made
a pilgrimage to England to see him, while Joséphin Péladan, the co-
founder and spiritual leader of the most famous of the Parisian
"Rosicrucian Lodges," easily out-performed him even on his own
ground, becoming a hack writer of awesome prolificity.  Péladan produced, among many other works, a fourteen-volume cycle of novels
collectively entitled *La Décadence latine* (1884-1906), and an eight-
volume guide to the *Amphithéatre des sciences mortes* (1892-1911).

Compared with such excesses as these, the limits of Bulwer's
ideological self-indulgence were both narrow and oddly perverse.  He
interrupted the relentless flow of his commercial three-volume novels in
1871 to issue an anonymous one-volume work, *The Coming Race*,
which describes the ambiguously Utopian world of the Vril-ya, who
have mastered the underlying force which is the essence of Nature's
Necessity, *vril*.  Although the work proved reasonably popular,
prompting Bulwer to own up to its authorship, its philosophical pretensions were not taken seriously and its most enduring effect has proved
to be the inspiration it lent to the manufacturers of Bovril.  When Bulwer's son, the Earl of Lytton, produced a credulous occult melodrama
called *The Ring of Amasis* (1863), he declared that it was unworthy of
the family name and insisted that it be issued under the pseudonym
Owen Meredith (although the young Earl reissued an abridged version
of it under his own name once the elder Lord Lytton was safely dead).

\* \* \* \* \* \* \*

*The Last Days of Pompeii* has been kept alive by modern reprints, but the spirit of the text was entirely lost in several attempts to recreate the eruption of Vesuvius in more spectacular media. A dire Hollywood film made in 1935 was followed by an even direr Italian "epic" starring the muscular Steve Reeves in 1959, both of which moved the unimportant gladiatorial sub-plot of the novel to center stage. A TV "mini-series" made in the 1980s stuck closer to the text, but could not capture the least hint of the crucial ambivalence of the character of Arbaces.

Like the pent-up wrath of Vesuvius, Bulwer's true feelings seethe far beneath the narrative surface of the novel, regretfully and resentfully demonized. "The character of Arbaces," the text observes in Chapter VIII of Book II,

> was one of those intricate and varied webs, in which
> even the mind which sat within it was sometimes con-
> fused and perplexed. In him, the son of a fallen dy-
> nasty, the outcast of a sunken people, was that spirit
> of discontented pride, which ever rankles in one of a
> sterner mould who feels himself inexorably shut from
> the sphere in which his fathers shone, and to which
> nature as well as birth no less entitled himself. This
> sentiment hath no benevolence; it wars with society, it
> sees enemies in mankind.

Bulwer's own disinheritance proved, in the end, to be tempo-rary, and he was well-sustained in the meantime by the prostitution of his aristocratic wit and wisdom to the reading tastes of the aspiring middle class, who took a snobbish pride in adopting what they took to be aristocratic values and affectations. His battle against adversity was closely run, but only for a while; he had already reverted to being a rich Tory by the time the railways swept his literary work to new fame and extravagant fortune. It is interesting to wonder, however, what Bulwer might have become if his mother had lived for ten or twenty more years, and kept Knebworth out of his possession indefinitely. The break with his aristocratic roots might then have become decisive, his radical sympathies might have intensified rather than fading away, and his "discontented pride" might have been fully liberated.

The passage cited above extends its analysis of Arbaces's char-acter at great and self-indulgent length. "The conscience of Arbaces was solely of the intellect," Bulwer observes in fascinated fashion, "it was awed by no moral laws. If man imposed these checks upon the herd, so he believed that man, by superior wisdom, could raise himself above them."

Bulwer was clearly tempted by such a prospect; unlike Apae-cides he was no natural ascetic, and he had no innate attraction to the

65

kind of Christianity which could rejoice in the belief that the apocalypse had come and that the Kingdom of Heaven was at hand.  In the fullness of time, though, he dutifully fell into step with the expectations of his milieu and his moment, just as he forced Glaucus to fall into step with the pious expectations of his readers.  We can only speculate as to whether this was really a happy ending from his point of view, but there can be few modern commentators who find the craven capitulation preferable to the glorious rebellion that might have been.

# VII.

# *VICE VERSA*

*Vice Versa; or, A Lesson to Fathers* by "F. Anstey," which was first published in 1882, has proved to be one of the most durable of all bestsellers. The various adaptations for the stage, the cinema, and TV which have kept it in the public eye have, however, wrought a gradual transformation of its content. *Vice Versa* is a work sustained by the strength of its central idea—a personality-exchange by means of which a father and his son find themselves inhabiting one another's bodies—and part of the strength of that idea is that it lends itself to constant updating while retaining all of its innate fascination. The original is a quintessentially Victorian fantasy, but the most recent film version, made in 1988 starring Judge Reinhold and Fred Savage, finds no difficulty in transplanting the premise to a modern American setting.

Although it was by no means the first literary account of an identity-exchange, *Vice Versa* was the first to use that device to explore the conflict of attitudes and interests characteristic of different social positions in a relatively even-handed way. Earlier stories in the same vein had focused on the awful disorientation suffered by a single displaced persona, or on the alleged futility of the notion that one might be better off living someone else's life. The comic potential of the notion had been explored in Robert MacNish's novelette "The Metempsychosis" (1826; originally signed "A Modern Pythagorean"), but not in any extended fashion. Longer works dealing with the transmigration theme had paid little or no attention to the reciprocity of the exchange, and tended to be more philosophically-inclined; the most notable example is Théophile Gautier's novella "Avatar" (1856). The author of *Vice Versa* was able to capitalize on the relative familiarity of the idea to move on to the next logical stage, patiently comparing and contrasting the joys and miseries which result when the minds of an adult and a child are embodied in inappropriate bodies. As might be expected, the boy initially finds more advantages in the exchange than the man, but he eventually decides that the natural order of things had better be restored.

The superficial moral of *Vice Versa* is, of course, that we all ought to be content to occupy our rightful places in society. What other conclusion could any Victorian fantasy be expected to reach? There is, however, a more subversive subtext in the novel which delights in the undignified imprisonment of the father and the marvellous liberation of the son. Although the son ultimately, and unsurprisingly, proves incapable of making full and happy use of his opportunity to taste the fruits of adulthood, it nevertheless remains a glorious liberation. Because the social positions of the two identity-exchangers are far from equal, the distribution of their miseries is dramatically unequal—and the story therefore has a second moral which runs in a contradictory direction to the more obvious one. *Vice Versa* is an essentially amiable book, with no trace of an iron fist lurking within its velvet glove, but it has claws of a kind, which deftly scratch away at the surface of thinly-armored prejudices.

Many other writers were to take up the subversive thread of *Vice Versa*, using identity-exchanges as a means of exploring the iniquities of social inequality. *Vice Versa* itself is little more than a sustained and scathing demolition of the nostalgic and oppressive adult-produced myth that one's schooldays are the happiest days of one's life, but its formula was capable of many further variations, as well as adaptation to map future change in the pattern of father/son relationships.

Works wholly or partly inspired by *Vice Versa* extend over a considerable spectrum, both in tone and in the specific relationships which they scrutinize, but they all carry similarly subversive subtexts, and the more earnest of them bring their subtexts into sharp focus. Examples range from such relatively slight and straightforward comic imitations as "The Great Keinplatz Experiment" (1885; professor and student) by Arthur Conan Doyle and "The Strange Adventure of Roger Wilkins" (1895; employer and employee) by "R. Andom" (Alfred W. Barrett), to such weighty and heavy-handed moralistic fantasies as *The Doubts of Dives* (1889; rich man and poor man) by Walter Besant and *The Ealing Miracle* (1911; middle-class woman and "bad" girl) by Horace W. C. Newte. The one kind of body-swap which was potentially more interesting than the father/son exchange had, of course, to wait for standards of literary decency to be relaxed, and had even then to be treated relatively coyly, in *Turnabout* (1931; husband and wife) by Thorne Smith.

In spite of the subversive nature of the subtexts carried by stories of this kind, it is notable that very few of them refuse the climactic restoration of the status quo. Anstey, who was a conservative through and through in spite of his penchant for poking fun at the pretensions of his era, would never have considered such a move. *Vice Versa* presents a fine caricature of the Victorian man of business in the character of Mr. Paul Bultitude, and merrily heaps a plague of humiliations upon him while he is trapped in his son's body at an appalling preparatory school, but the story is devoid of any real animosity. The author never doubts for an instant that a bourgeois Victorian gentleman is the best thing in the world to be, and it is not surprising that so many fathers were happy to take their lesson in good part.

Having said this, though, it must also be observed that Anstey's narrative does dwell rather self-indulgently on the sheer horror of the elder Bultitude's predicament, and it does have some force as a straightforward revenge fantasy. Like all comedy, the comedy of Ansteyan fantasy has a slightly nasty streak, which is not completely masked by the friendly smile it wears.

* * * * * * *

"F. Anstey" was the pseudonym of Thomas Anstey Guthrie, who was the son of a military tailor. He was born in 1856, just before the mid-point of Victoria's long reign, and was very much a product of that era. He intended to sign his work T. Anstey, but the typesetter of his first published short story, "Accompanied on the Flute" (1878), made a mistake and the author accepted the judgment of fate with characteristic good humor. In his posthumously-published autobiography, *A Long Retrospect* (1936), he remarked in an off-hand manner that he had never bothered to decide what the F was supposed to stand for. In the same volume he steadfastly refused to identify the preparatory school which furnished him with the background for *Vice Versa*, or to name its tyrannical headmaster, although it could hardly have done any harm to do so after half a century had passed. He did, however, take pains to insist that certain seemingly-unlikely episodes in the novel (the dictated letter home is a classic) were drawn with perfect accuracy from life.

From preparatory school Guthrie went to King's College School and eventually to Trinity Hall, Cambridge, where he read law. *Vice Versa* was begun and half-completed while he was still an undergraduate, but he put it aside when the death of his mother robbed him of his appetite for comedy. His first two stories, both published in the short-lived periodical *Mirth*, were non-fantastic comedies that drew on his classical education, but he found a more productive vein in his parodies of the popular ghost stories of the day, "The Wraith of Barnjum" (1879) and "The Curse of the Catafalques" (1882). His other early stories were sickly-sentimental stories of childhood—"The Sugar Prince" (1880) is an appropriately-titled example about a confection with delusions of nobility. He always considered himself to be gifted with a special insight into the world of children's experience, although he only wrote one book specifically aimed at juvenile readers and never had any children of his own; indeed, he never married, becoming a paradigm example of that now-extinct but then-honored stereotype, the confirmed bachelor.

At first, *Vice Versa* met a distinctly cool reception from publishers, but the magazine-editor and humorist James Payn persuaded

69

George Smith of Smith, Elder & Co to take a chance with it. Smith paid £25 for the copyright and promised the author a further £25 if the book were ever reprinted, but he felt guilty enough after its runaway success to pay out a further £500. Although Guthrie had by then been called to the bar, he promptly gave up the law and became a man of letters. His ambition was to become a serious novelist, but in the event his earnest works failed dismally, and his reputation came to rest entirely on his comic writings; he earned his living primarily as a member of the regular stable of writers supplying material to *Punch*.

"F. Anstey" was never able to repeat the runaway success of *Vice Versa*, and always regretted the fact. His serious novels were not nearly as good as he certainly hoped and perhaps believed—the first of them, *The Giant's Robe* (1884), is so ponderously mannered and pompously moralistic that it would surely never have been published had it not had a best-selling name attached to it—but some of his subsequent comic fantasies were both better-written and more substantial than *Vice Versa*. Like other writers before him, though, Anstey found that the Victorians preferred their comedies and their fantasies to be determinedly insubstantial. Even Charles Dickens had failed to recapitulate the popular success of *A Christmas Carol* (1843) in weightier moral fantasies like "The Chimes" (1844) and "The Haunted Man and the Ghost's Bargain" (1848), because his public much preferred the cozy and unthreatening sentimentality of "A Cricket on the Hearth" (1845); poor Anstey had no chance of succeeding where Dickens had failed.

Anstey's settlement into the specialism of comic fantasy was gradual and grudging. His second comic novel, *A Tinted Venus* (1885), was commissioned by the Bristol-based publisher Arrowsmith, who specialized in slim volumes of "pocket-book" dimensions. It begins promisingly enough, but peters out feebly; this was partly because the nature of the commission required a modest word-length, but also, one suspects, because the ominous subtext threatened to overtake and overwhelm the light comedy. *The Tinted Venus* is one of several notable fantasies based on an anecdote in Robert Burton's *Anatomy of Melancholy*, about a statue of Aphrodite which comes to life after a ring is placed on the finger in accidental imitation of a betrothal ceremony. Victorian hairdresser Leander Tweddle inevitably finds the amorous goddess a terrible embarrassment, but Anstey could only flirt very delicately with the erotic implications, and in the end refused to follow up the more sinister aspects of the reincarnate Aphrodite's plans.

*A Fallen Idol* (1886), in which a young artist falls under the baleful influence of a statue infused by the spirit of a fake holy man mistakenly elevated to godhood, is not so half-hearted. It develops the element of unease much more strongly, resulting in some passages of authentic horror. It certainly has claims to be considered Anstey's best book, but the audience seemed not to relish this development; the critical reception of the book was cool. Anstey seems to have tried thereafter to keep the darker element in his work under a tight rein, although it resurfaces constantly and was eventually to move to center-stage in some of his later and briefer paranoid fantasies, most notably "The Lights of Spencer Primmett's Eyes" (1896) and "Ferdie" (1907).

In 1887 Anstey "joined the *Punch* table" (the staff of the magazine enjoyed a ritual dinner in the office every Wednesday). The salary he was paid allowed him space to write another serious novel, *The Pariah* (1889), but it fared no better than *The Giant's Robe*. He was on the staff of the magazine for ten years, and became such a popular fixture in its pages that he was allowed to retain his precious seat at the table for some years after he reverted to irregular contributions paid on a piecework basis.

Most of the books Anstey published while he drew his salary from *Punch* were based on his work for the magazine, but he did write one more fantasy novel: a notable early time-paradox story called *Tourmalin's Time Cheques* (1891; later reprinted as *The Time Bargain*). This relates the adventures of a young man faced with the tedious prospect of a sea voyage from Sydney to London, who accepts an offer made by a fellow-passenger to "deposit" the journey-time in a "bank." He finds himself immediately at home, in possession of a cheque-book with which he may redeem the deposited time by the hour whenever he wishes to enjoy a brief respite from his daily routine. Unfortunately, the hours which he reclaims are out of sequence, and he soon discovers that the voyage was much more eventful than he had anticipated. Complications multiply rapidly, until the interest earned by his deposit begins to overlap time through which he has already lived. Ingenious and delightful though it was, the book was not successful.

\* \* \* \* \* \* \*

Guthrie tried yet again to gain recognition as a serious novelist when he produced *The Statement of Stella Maberly* (1896), publishing it anonymously so as not to prejudice the expectations of his readers. Like his earlier novels it is a story of intense psychological pressure, in this case exaggerated to the point where it results in mental abnormality. Although it was considerably better than its predecessors, its sales were even lower. Guthrie acknowledged defeat at this point, and immediately reverted to being F. Anstey, accepting all that the name implied. He never wrote another earnest book, although the quirky romantic novella *Love Among the Lions* (1898) is by no means a wholehearted comedy. His autobiography is scrupulously philosophical about his failure to produce a successful serious work, but the bitter disappointment of that failure is not entirely veiled. It is hardly surprising that his next full-length project involved a calculated return to the formula which had served him best, nor that its skillful execution brought him his second-greatest success.

*The Brass Bottle* (1900) describes the adventures of Horace Ventimore, who liberates a jinnee from the eponymous object, which he purchases by accident at an auction. The jinnee is so grateful that he wants to make Horace the richest man in the world and gratify his every whim, but his efforts can cause nothing but embarrassment to a young man whose sole desire is to retreat into inconspicuous middle-class responsibility with his wife-to-be. The jinnee, seeing his finest gifts spurned and wasted, ultimately becomes impatient with his rescuer's ingratitude, and Horace is forced to use his wits rather more cleverly than the sailor in the famous tale from the *Thousand-and-One Nights* who confronted a more straightforward threat from a less intelligent adversary.

Anstey must have had high hopes for his children's book *Only Toys* (1902), but it fell victim to disaster when the publisher went bankrupt immediately prior to its release; the copies were remaindered by the receiver without ever having been offered to the public at the full price. The story bears some relation to the manifest moral of *Vice Versa*, in that it counsels children against being too eager to emerge from the nursery into the adult world. Its two protagonists, told that they are "growing out" of their toys, ask Santa Claus to reduce them in size so that they may re-enter the toys' world as equals. Unfortunately, the toys prove unrewarding companions, and the children are ungrateful; Santa Claus is moved to punish this ingratitude by making the toys "more human"—which is to say, domineering, greedy, and aggressive. The lesson which the children subsequently learn is sharp enough, although its moral propriety is not entirely clear.

In the early years of the twentieth century Anstey had rather more luck as a playwright than as a novelist. One of his Punch pieces, "The Man from Blankley's" was successfully, if somewhat belatedly, adapted for the stage in 1901 (the script had been written in 1893), and Anstey subsequently produced dramatic versions of many other works, including *The Brass Bottle* (1909) and *Vice Versa* (1910). It was through his association with the theatre that he eventually won a measure of the respectability he had long craved, and he devoted the last years of his life (he died in 1934) to the adaptation for the English stage of various plays by Molière. He wrote only one more novel, *In Brief Authority* (1915), which was very poorly received in spite of the fact that it ranks alongside *A Fallen Idol* as one of the most interesting of his works.

*In Brief Authority* reverses the strategy of Anstey's earlier fantasies. Instead of bringing a single magical object into the highly-ordered world of the respectable middle class, it displaces a "typical" middle-class family into a magical land. It is perhaps unfortunate that the Great War broke out while the book was in production, given that the magical land in question is explicitly Germanic, based on the *märchenland* of the Brothers Grimm.

The satirical edge which was carefully blunted in Anstey's earlier novels is more finely-honed in *In Brief Authority*. The matron of the family to which the central characters belong is a hypocritical, self-deluding, and thoroughly stupid snob who accepts an heirloom from one of her servants as security for a loan. Her possession of this object wrongly identifies her to emissaries from *märchenland* as their rightful queen.. Her blinkered determination to import British social niceties into their barbaric realm nearly results in disaster, and the revelation that the humble and compassionate servant is in fact the true monarch comes just in time to avert actual and moral chaos.

In *A Long Retrospect* Anstey wrote off the failure of *In Brief Authority* with the suggestion that the time for his kind of humor had passed, but the continued activity of several imitators calls this conclusion into question, as does the success of a 1931 omnibus of his most popular works, *Humour and Fantasy*. It is more probable that, as with *A Fallen Idol*, the novel's sharpness made too many readers feel uncomfortable, refusing to let their pretensions and prejudices off the hook as easily as the conscientiously amiable *Vice Versa* had.

\* \* \* \* \* \* \*

There is a sense in which the particular species of humor featured in F. Anstey's novels was bound to go out of fashion following the end of the Victorian era. The stubborn rigidity of social conventions and the fiercely exacting pressure of middle-class mores which encapsulated the spirit of the great queen's reign had inevitably to be relaxed when they had run their unreasonable course. As those strictures weakened, the extreme opposition between their perfervid uptightness and the anarchic mischief-making powers which Anstey imputed to pagan magic was gradually lost. The points which Anstey scored against the pomposity, self-congratulation, and bigotry of the Victorians came eventually to seem too easy, and the fact that he retained a light touch while getting his digs in came to be seen as a weakness rather than a strength.

Although his personal resentments and frustrations were always evident in his work, even when they were submerged, Anstey was too sensible—and too polite—to agonize about them. Many later writers were by no means so restrained. Those British humorists who preserved a polite amiability similar to Anstey's rarely toyed, as Anstey frequently did, with any real opposition to the values their characters embodied and upheld; those who were not so polite felt freer to indulge the naked hostility which he had so patiently clothed.

It is worth noting that *Laughing Gas* (1936), the sole fantasy novel written by P. G. Wodehouse, the leading politely-humorous writer of the post-Ansteyan era, is an identity-exchange story clearly inspired by *Vice Versa*. It involves a typically-eccentric English aristocrat and a spoiled but streetwise brat whose ego has been monstrously inflated by his status as a terminally cute movie-star. Other British writers of Ansteyan fantasy mostly steered clear of the identity-ex-change motif. The most successful of them, W. A. Darlington, substi-tuted a comic cockney straight out of Anstey's long-running *Punch* feature *Voces Populi* for the more respectable heroes of Anstey's novels in a series of sketches which were ultimately rewritten into the best-selling *Alf's Button* (1919). Darlington's attempts to make light of the Great War were evidently welcome at the time, although they seem slightly sick to modern readers who know the truth which was carefully hidden by the military censors; his later novels in the same vein were far less popular.

It is not altogether surprising that the most successful updating of Ansteyan fantasy was not carried out in Britain at all, but in the US, where a different brand of absurd uptightness reached its peak in the era of the Volstead Act. The American writer Thorne Smith was able to take up where Anstey had left off partly because he was able to flirt much more audaciously with matters of sexuality. He also was able to celebrate the magically-liberating effects of booze in collaboration with an audience which had witnessed the woefully unanticipated and ironi-cally unfortunate effects of its prohibition. In today's conscientiously liberal society there is much less scope for the effective use of Ansteyan fantasy, because there are very few social taboos which retain sufficient strength to provide worthy opposition to mischievous magic. Only children, it seems, nowadays live in a world rigidly bound by limits which are as patently unreasonable as they are oppressive, licensing the production of new Ansteyan fantasies for a juvenile audience—and, of course, the constant updating of *Vice Versa* for new generations.

On the other hand, it might be noted that there never has been a competent reprise of Thorne Smith's *Turnabout*. One suspects that this is not because the inequalities of contemporary men and women are too trivial to warrant such examination, but rather because a thorough treatment of them would inevitably tend to the pornographic. Perhaps there is scope here for a modern Anstey, who might just be able to bring off the trick of combining polite amiability with some sharply subversive commentary on the current state of play in the ongoing war of the sexes. There have been several moderately-effective timeslip fantasies of a feminist stripe, and it may be only a matter of time before a notable feminist variant of the theme of *Vice Versa* appears; the mother/daughter identity-exchange featured in the film, *Freaky Friday* (1977) represents a step in that direction.

Whether a modern *Turnabout* could revitalize Ansteyan fantasy for adult readers remains to be seen, but it might be foolish to be over-optimistic. It would surely require a writer of considerable skill to em-ulate Anstey in preventing such an exercise from collapsing into a mere horror story or a non-vintage whine.

# VIII.

# MARIE CORELLI

When Sigmund Freud set out to explain the hidden logic of dreams, he began by making the the bold assertion that all dreams, however peculiar or disturbing they may be, are really adventures in wish-fulfillment. He was probably wrong about the kind of dreams which visit us by night, but if we are to speak of the kind of dreams which are carefully constructed as stories and avidly consumed by millions of readers, then the claim is much safer. Bestsellers are exercises in wish-fulfillment which gratify the unfulfilled, intimate, and sometimes secret desires which are common to the hearts of large numbers of people.

Oddly enough, it is not always easy to figure out why certain books become bestsellers. Some of our desires are perfectly obvious, but many of them are not. We routinely conceal many of our yearnings, and hold them in check, sometimes because it would be antisocial or impolite to express them, and sometimes because they are too tender and too precious to be exposed to the possibility of ridicule. There is nothing more private and personal than our daydreams, and no one really knows how common or how rare his own daydreams are. Nor do we know ourselves well enough to be always certain what it is that we yearn for when we feel empty or dissatisfied—and we may not know, even if we are lucky enough to find it, why it was what we needed. For these reasons, the success of some bestsellers comes as a complete surprise to everyone, and remains an awkward puzzle to those in search of explanations.

Marie Corelli was one of the most surprising and most puzzling bestsellers of all time. For ten or fifteen years around the turn of the last century she was the most popular writer in the English language, and no one—least of all the contemporary critics and reviewers, who despised her work—could figure out why. Her own answer (that she was a great genius who was attacked by reviewers only because they were envious of her greatness) was dismissed out of hand, although she clung to it very tenaciously; she made of her own life story a fantastic tissue of lies and conceits every bit as absurd and grotesque as those she penned. Indisputably, though, she touched some hidden chord in her readers, and gave them something which was exactly right to fill a hidden void inside them.

After Marie Corelli's death, when it was no longer possible for any libel action to be brought against it, the *News of the World* tried to expose the "truth" behind her masquerade, following its own customary formula for pandering to the desires of its readers, but the story in question was only one more sad and spiteful fantasy, adding to the mystery instead of solving it.

Marie Corelli's books are no longer read; no one nowadays can find anything personally rewarding in her works, although they still have a certain fascination as specimens of an extinct point of view. This, too, is a puzzle of sorts. It informs us that a covert, unfulfilled desire which millions of people once had has vanished utterly, presumably never to return. It reminds us, in fact, that the past really is a foreign country, where they not only do things differently, but also feel things differently. Because books like Marie Corelli's survive, however, the past is a country we can still visit, as tourists of the imagination, in order to to marvel, to wonder, and to try to understand.

\* \* \* \* \* \* \*

Marie Corelli lied about her name, age, and origins so insistently that her true history still remains somewhat clouded. At some time in the 1860s she appeared, as a young girl, in the household of the poet Charles Mackay. He adopted her, and she was thereafter known by the name of Minnie Mackay. She always denied that Mackay was her natural father, but the likelihood is that she was his illegitimate daughter, borne by his one-time servant Mary Mills, probably in 1855. Mackay had married Mary Mills in 1861, a few years before Minnie was formally welcomed into the family.

Charles Mackay apparently doted upon his adopted daughter and encouraged her to believe that she was unusually gifted. His attempts to pass her off as a brilliant pianist came to nothing, and her first literary efforts were rejected, but her self-confidence was quite undented by this lack of wider appreciation; throughout her life she remained utterly incapable of doubting herself.

When Mary Mackay died in 1876, she was replaced in the household by Bertha Vyver, a girl of about the same age as Minnie, who remained her companion and most devout admirer for the rest of her life. When Charles Mackay was paralyzed by a stroke in 1884, he too was replaced in the little community by his son from his first marriage, Eric, who also had pretensions to be a poet. Eric flattered Minnie as much as his father had, though probably for more cynical reasons. When she became successful, she supported him in idleness and paid for the publication of his works, although she was apparently deeply shocked to discover, after his death in 1898, how much of her money he had spent on prostitutes.

It was also in 1884 that "Marie Corelli" was invented, the name being applied to poems which she submitted to various literary magazines. She claimed that it was her true name, and embellished her letters of submission with extravagant stories about her imagined Italian origins. It was the name under which she wrote her first full-length book, *A Romance of Two Worlds*, which is set in 1884 and features as its unnamed heroine exactly the kind of person that Marie Corelli was supposed by her inventor to be: gifted, exotic, sensitive, but as yet unable to fulfill her abundant promise because of an unfortunate weakness of body and spirit, and because other people are too crass to appreciate her true worth.

*A Romance of Two Worlds* is not really a novel. It is a first-person account of an amazing religious revelation, full of forceful essays in theology and morality, the unorthodoxy of the former being excused by the rigorous conventionality of the latter. The faith which it propounds is a strange hybrid of pious Christianity and the fashionable pseudosciences of the day, which sets out to rationalize belief in the soul by means of a theory of "human electricity." The text's fundamental purpose is to rescue a religious faith in decline by recruiting the language of science to "prove" its essential truth. This is accomplished by presenting an exemplary story in which the young narrator—who is, after the fashion of romantic heroines, attractive though not "conventionally" beautiful—comes to fascinate in turn an exotic painter, a charismatic occultist, and one of God's own angels.

The heroine's potential is first recognized by the painter Raffaello Cellini, who can produce realistic images of the angels by virtue of his acquaintance with the Chaldean mystic Casimir Heliobas. Heliobas is first introduced to the heroine through the medium of visions, but he comes to her in the flesh soon enough. Once this meeting has been contrived, and the heroine's spiritual worthiness established, Heliobas infuses her with the human electricity which is the substance of which souls are made, renewing her physical and spiritual strength. Thus equipped with boundless self-confidence, she becomes fit company for the angels, and goes with one of them on a conducted tour of the universe, effortlessly penetrating its deepest mysteries. She learns, among other things, that the inhabitants of all other worlds are much happier than the men and women of earth, because no other planet is so deeply steeped in sin and its consequent miseries. Eventually, she is allowed to see God in His true form, as a "Great Circle of Electric Fire."

*A Romance of Two Worlds* was bought by George Bentley, who published it in 1886 despite having certain misgivings about its absurd pretensions. The reviews which it received were scathing, mocking the ludicrousness of the plot and castigating its literary style, but the reading public responded very differently. The book sold well, and found some enthusiastic champions among the great and the good, including William Gladstone and Queen Victoria; the author's delusions of grandeur were thus made permanently secure.

It is not so very difficult to see what the elder statesman and the aged queen found to admire in *A Romance of Two Worlds*. They were both steadfast champions of a stern morality, earnest poseurs who tried to make examples for others to follow out of the conduct of their own lives; in Marie Corelli they recognized another very like themselves, prepare to man the barricades against the forces of corruption which were massed on all sides. Despite its theological unorthodoxy, *A Romance of Two Worlds* was clamorous in its support of the piously repressive morality whose symbolic figurehead Queen Victoria had become, and if the means needed justifying, that end was widely held to be justification enough. Marie Corelli became the last great popular champion of a Victorianism which was already in decline, and she provided an ideological life raft for many of those who were deeply anxious and mordantly regretful about its passing.

Throughout her career Marie Corelli was to remain utterly obsessive in her unqualified support for such Victorian shibboleths as the supreme importance of chastity and marital fidelity, and the transcendent nature of true love. She was equally obsessive in her vitriolic hatred for the enemies whose war of attrition was casting those idols down, and in her ever-readiness to attack the moral corruptness of aristocratic society and the vileness of the press. The spread of more tolerant attitudes always harden the intolerance of those who do not hold them, and the late Victorians who took advantage of the relaxation of standards were attacked and vilified by the old guard for their "decadence." In France, a movement was emerging of artists who were proud and glad to accept and wear that label, but when the movement was imported into Britain in the 1890s—when Marie Corelli's career was at its spectacular height—it met much fiercer opposition. That opposition precipitated a feverish backlash of outrage, which culminated in the malevolent persecution and calculated degradation of Oscar Wilde.

Ironically, Wilde was one of the few reviewers who declined the opportunity to heap derision on *A Romance of Two Worlds*, finding something to praise—albeit rather faintly—in its vaulting imagination. Wilde was one of the few readers capable of recognizing that the novel actually had strong affinities with certain French works, especially the novels of the would-be Rosicrucian magus Joséphin Péladan, which similarly feature charismatic mystics bent on saving the world from the fatal corruptions of a loss of religious faith. Péladan found evidence of the decadence of the modern world everywhere, and was enthusiastic to sound a clarion call for a new Renaissance; but his readers appreciated his lavish descriptions of decadence far more than his insistently ridiculous recipes for its cure. In Britain Marie Corelli not only found an audience very willing to share her sense of horror at the way the world was going, but one that was willing to sympathize with her accounts of the extreme and desperate measures that might be necessary to its salvation.

\* \* \* \* \* \* \*

George Bentley did his best to limit the sillier ambitions of his unexpected bestseller. He advised her to abandon her philosophical pretensions and her supernatural apparatus, and write books which could pass muster as conventional novels. At first she consented to be advised, restraining her ambitions in the melodrama *Vendetta* (1886) and the love story *Thelma* (1887), but the notion that she had become the vehicle of a new revelation capable of saving the world was nourished by letters from readers of *A Romance of Two Worlds* (some of which she reproduced in later printings of the book), who claimed to have been rescued by it from the pit of despair. Inevitably, she soon set out on a new philosophical masterpiece, *Ardath* (1889), in which Heliobas returned to work new miracles, this time on behalf of a male protagonist loosely (probably far more loosely than she supposed) based on her half-brother, to whom the book is unctuously dedicated.

Like the heroine of *A Romance of Two Worlds*, the hero of *Ardath* is not only recruited to the side of the angels, but also to their company. After falling in love with one, he is sent back through time to the city of Al-Kyris, which allegedly thrived five thousand years before Christ, where he meets an earlier incarnation of himself and eventually proves himself worthy of his ideal. Never one for half-measures, the author permits the man and the angel to undergo an actual wedding ceremony in one of Europe's great cathedrals.

Bentley did not like *Ardath* at all, and bravely suffered the outrage and wrath of the author after saying so, but he published it and it sold in vast quantities. Again he advocated restraint, and again Marie Corelli consented to be restrained, after a fashion. Her next novel, *Wormwood* (1890), addressed the subject of French Decadence directly, describing in a surprisingly convincing fashion the degradation of a man sucked into a Parisian underworld of absinthe dens and brothels. It was followed, however, by another exercise in mysticism, even more earnest and more ponderous than those which had gone before, entitled *The Soul of Lilith* (1892).

Marie Corelli finally exhausted her publisher's patience with her ambitions and affectations when she released an anonymous work called *The Silver Domino*, a scurrilous "exposé" of high-society mores which contained thinly-veiled portraits of several actual people, including the Prince of Wales. This was one of several attempts which she made to score a point off the critics, who continued to be merciless

# Marie Corelli

in making fun of her books; she thought it the kind of thing they would approve of, and hoped that they would praise it, so that she prove that their regular attacks on her capabilities as a writer were nothing but personal malice. In fact, it was as unkindly reviewed as anything else she had done, and she had to be content to let it remain anonymous, but George Bentley knew that she was responsible for it, and he disapproved strongly enough to let her go to another publisher. His disapproval cost him dear, for the period of her greatest success was just beginning.

\* \* \* \* \* \* \*

*Barabbas* (1893) was probably the most successful of all Marie Corelli's books, and it remains the best-known. Like most of her other works, it tells the story of a man redeemed from potentially-fatal and spiritually-disfiguring scepticism by a religious revelation, but it eschews the fashionable mysticism of her earlier fantasies and ambitiously selects as its hero a key character from the New Testament.

The critics complained that *Barabbas* was woefully inaccurate as a depiction of first-century life, gleefully pointing out what they considered to be schoolboy howlers (particularly the fact that the hero's sister is also surnamed Barabbas, an error which allowed mockers to recall the narrator's casual assertion in *A Romance of Two World* that the surname of the painter of the Sistine Chapel ceiling was Angelo), but the author's faithful readers did not care a fig about such minor matters. For them, the authenticity of the book was entirely contained in its sentiment, which expressed in no uncertain terms the opinion that only a fierce commitment to the Christian faith can make human life worth living. In *Barabbas* Marie Corelli spoke to her readers in much the same way that televangelists nowadays speak to their viewers, and with much the same result (although she seems to have been a good deal more conscientious in practising what she preached).

*Barabbas* was followed by another extravagant fantasy, which similarly sought to break new ground, and which similarly became a runaway bestseller. This was *The Sorrows of Satan* (1895), which revealed that even the archenemy of mankind was secretly on the side of the angels. Blake had long ago alleged that Milton was of the devil's party without knowing it, and in his wake had come numerous Romantic poets who found something to admire in Lucifer's rebellion against the tyranny of God; Marie Corelli, in her own inimitable fashion, turned this notion on its head. Her Satan has already repented his rebellion, and longs for the day when mankind will begin to resist the temptations which he lays before them, at which time even he might be forgiven and redeemed. Geoffrey Tempest, the male protagonist of the novel, is far too easily recruited to the cause of his own damnation to give the Devil any shred of hope, but in the course of attending to

80

Tempest's corruption, Satan is fortunate enough to meet the saintly novelist Mavis Clare, with whose indomitable incorruptibility he inevitably falls in love. Marie Corelli, with typically-awesome false modesty, stoutly denied that Mavis Clare had been intended as a self-portrait, but no one believed her.

It was in *The Sorrows of Satan* that Marie Corelli reached the pinnacle of her unique literary achievement. No other writer had ever dared credit herself with sufficient goodness and glamour to win the sincere love of the Devil himself, thereby renewing the hope that the Prince of Darkness might eventually be saved. As delusions of grandeur and expressions of devout wish-fulfillment go, this was an unsurpassable masterstroke. The author continued to churn out bestsellers, but there was no further boundary to surpass, and it was all mere repetition. *The Mighty Atom* (1896) deserves attention as a rare tragic variation, which leaves its young hero unredeemed (driven to suicide, in fact, by the atheism which he is educated to accept), but her later novels became increasingly tired and lacklustre. A late fantasy of magical rejuvenation, *The Young Diana* (1918), is undermined by the fact that the author had all too obviously lost faith—as, in time, everyone does—in the achievability of her most ardent desires.

The enervation of Marie Corelli's later novels was mirrored by disappointments in real life, which added to the burden of growing old. She always pretended to be younger than she was, but her body was less adept in supporting the lie than she could have wished. Soon after the death of Charles Mackay she moved to Stratford-upon-Avon, accompanied by Bertha Vyver. There she became besotted with the painter Arthur Severn, but he was happily married and not really fitted for the kind of flattering role which had earlier been played by her father and half-brother. She did not want him for a lover, of course—like the heroines of her novels she felt that she was far too good for anyone but an angel, and probably died a virgin—but Platonic Adoration for a plain, short, fat, middle-aged poseur (as she then was) was similarly beyond Severn's capacities. She tried valiantly to boost his career, and used him as the hero of the most thoughtful of her later novels, *The Life Everlasting* (1910), but the old depth of feeling simply was not there.

Marie Corelli's popularity was on the wane from the turn of the century, though her celebrity continue to assure bestseller status for such novels as *The Master Christian* (1900), *God's Good Man* (1904), *The Treasure of Heaven* (1906), and *Holy Orders* (1908). The impetus of her earlier works was gone, and it never returned. By 1910 she was deemed to be an eccentric, fighting a battle which was already lost, although the remaindering of her early novels in the islands of the Caribbean, where they were frequently used as reading texts in schools, helped to maintain her reputation there for several decades more. Controversy never quite deserted her, however, and she made an unwelcome return to the newspaper headlines when she was arrested during the Great War on a charge of food-hoarding.

\* \* \* \* \* \* \*

*The News of the World* story which was published with indecent haste after her death alleged that "Marie Corelli" was actually the daughter of a London laborer, and that her real name—before her adoption by Charles Mackay—had been Caroline Cody. The evidence on which the claim was made was rather slight, but may be adequate to sustain the conclusion that she spent her earliest years, before she joined the Mackay household, with the Cody family. The likelihood is that she was placed there by her father so that he might make an honest woman of Mary Mills without undue embarrassment to himself or to her.

In the final analysis, it really does not matter very much whether Marie Corelli was born Caroline Cody or Minnie Mackay. She certainly became, as completely and as wholeheartedly as she possibly could, Marie Corelli. She remade herself in an image which she considered most highly desirable, and she used her novels to encourage her readers to believe that they, too, might remake themselves. Nor was her aim in remaking herself entirely selfish; she was sincerely interested in the salvation of the world from its presumed misery and degradation. The nonsense which she wrote, however inept it may have been in literary and philosophical terms, was honest nonsense.

We all feel compelled to draw a curtain of privacy across our most cherished daydreams, and we have several good reasons for so doing. Some must be hidden from the scrutiny of others lest they be thought obscene or offensive, but others must be hidden simply because they would seem too naïve and unsophisticated. Marie Corelli did not consider herself naïve or unsophisticated, because she had somehow learned to be utterly unashamed to hold opinions and indulge fantasies that others considered imbecilic. She was prepared to expose to the world the stupid sophistry by which she tried to shore up her religious faith with borrowed jargon, and her narcissistic fantasies of being more suited for the company of angels than mere men. The astonishing success of her works demonstrates that her expression of her own delusions and aspirations were capable of soothing, at least in some small measure, the distress of millions of her contemporaries.

Having said this, one must of course add that the critics were entirely right about Marie Corelli. She was a bad writer from every possible objective point of view, and the morality which she espoused was as unreasonable as her ridiculous notion of human nature. The fact that she was able to supply a kind of opium to ease the pain of her countless admirers is a testament to the evils and misfortunes of the time in which she lived, not to her own genius. We have every reason to be glad that modern readers find her unreadable, because that fact informs us that our world has made some slight moral progress since the last zealots of Victorianism vented their angry and fearful desperation in the symbolic crucifixion of Oscar Wilde. We have our own bestsellers who are no less silly, no less convinced of their own genius, and who answer covert yearnings which are not one whit more laudable, but we have every reason to believe—or, at any rate, to hope—that they too will find their popularity waning as the march of progress renders them unnecessary.

# IX.

# *THE GARDEN OF ALLAH*

*The Garden of Allah* (1904) was published while Marie Corelli was still the most popular writer in Britain, and it must have seemed to many readers to be taking up where she was beginning to leave off. Like many of Miss Corelli's bestsellers, Robert Hichens's novel is a love story in which the extraordinary overheating of the central characters' passions is linked to the presumed intensity and grandiosity of religious experience. Hichens was not the only writer to ride to bestsellerdom on Marie Corelli's exotic coat-tails—Florence Barclay's *The Rosary* (1909) caught the same tide before it began to ebb—but he was the only one whose work warrants comparison with hers in terms of its oddity and its depth of feeling. This is curious, given that the two writers apparently had little else in common.

Hichens continued writing until his death in 1950, the year in which his last book, the short-story collection *The Man in the Mirror* was published, but he never again achieved the kind of popular success that *The Garden of Allah* enjoyed. Nor did he ever again produce anything as peculiarly exotic; his later books were considerably more conventional, and even the kindest critic would be obliged to admit that he became distinctly boring as he produced dozens of increasingly verbose and conspicuously uneventful novels. The work which Hichens published before *The Garden of Allah* is, by contrast, replete with intensely peculiar and eccentrically feverish texts, including one of the most frequently-reprinted Victorian ghost stories, "How Love Came to Professor Guildea." This material displays many of the same tensions and fascinations as *The Garden of Allah*, and may be seen in retrospect as a process of evolution towards what one can hardly help but see as a kind of cathartic discharge of the author's pent-up feelings.

The protagonist of *The Garden of Allah* is a young aristocratic Englishwoman, Domini Enfilden, who is travelling in North Africa. Her journey is no mere tourist trip; from the very beginning (when we encounter her reading Cardinal Newman's verse epic about the soul's journey to judgment, *The Dream of Gerontius*), it is represented as a kind of pilgrimage: a flight from the distractions of civilization in quest of some unspecifiable spiritual truth. The Sahara Desert—the "garden" of the title—features throughout the book as a quasi-supernatural landscape whose immanent godhead is more fundamental and less distorted than the supposedly-derivative images reflected in the major world religions and the pagan beliefs which they replaced.

The plot of the novel initially follows a pattern which has since been enshrined as the principal formula of mass-produced romantic fiction. Domini meets a man named Androvsky, whose behavior towards her is at first offensive and disdainful. She is attracted to him anyway, even though she glimpses in his eyes what appear to be "unfathomable depths of misery or of wickedness." She observes him secretly for some days, during which she notices that he has a curious aversion to priests and other symbols of religion.

The antagonism between Domini and Androvsky gradually changes into a fierce erotic attraction, which is mirrored in a whole series of fervent atmospheric effects. Carried away by their passion, they decide to be married—an undertaking which is conducted in frank defiance of Androvsky's antipathy to all religious symbols and ceremonies. This antipathy appears to be mutual; it is reflected not only in the dark suspicions of the local priest but in the literally ominous behavior of a silver crucifix which hangs in his church.

After their marriage, Domini and her husband go on into the deepest heart of the desert. Androvsky has in his possession a quantity of a liqueur called Louarine, which is recognized by a priest they happen across as the unique product of a particular Trappist monastery. The priest tells Domini that the secret of Louarine's manufacture is reserved by tradition to be the privilege of only one man, and that the most recent inheritor of this trust disappeared from the monastery, thus violating both his holy vows and his duty to confide the formula of the liqueur to a new custodian. Androvsky, of course, is that man. Androvsky eventually confesses his sin to Domini, and then to the priest who married them. Having purged himself of guilt and achieved true repentance, he returns whence he came, feeling that his love for Domini would be fatally diminished were he not to place honor ahead of it in the hierarchy of his affections.

Domini fully endorses Androvsky's decision. She is left to bring up their as-yet-unborn son alone, but she feels that everything has now been set to rights, and that her fierce spiritual hunger (which Freud and many others would interpret as sublimated sexual desire) has been fully and properly appeased. Although her story has extended far beyond the customary end-point of the conventional love-story formula, into literary territory previously unexplored by the pen of man or woman, Domini ultimately receives the same magical endowment of contentment.

\* \* \* \* \* \* \*

A cynical commentator might argue that there is little more going on in *The Garden of Allah* than an attempt to dignify and glorify the force of sexual attraction by ornamenting it with a fanciful kind of sanctity, as Marie Corelli had earlier done and Florence Barclay was later to do—and, for that matter, as Barbara Cartland, in her own slightly more muted fashion, still does to considerable commercial effect. The huge popular success of the book may indeed have had much to do with the ready market which exists for the aestheticization of lust, but simply to make that observation does not exhaust the fascination of the text. As with Miss Corelli, one is drawn to wonder about the secret fountainhead of the remarkable depth of feeling which the book displays. What disturbances of Hichens's soul could possibly have encouraged him to produce such a bizarre account of a pilgrim's progress towards tranquillity?

As in any such analysis, much must be left to speculation, but in Hichens's case—unlike Miss Corelli's—we do have the assistance of an autobiography, *Yesterday* (1947), which gives the impression of containing nothing but the truth, if perhaps not the whole truth.

Robert Hichens was born in 1864 in the village of Speldhurst in Kent. Like many other writers of imaginative fiction born in Victorian times, he was the son of a clergyman who abandoned his father's orthodox piety in favor of a more dilute and abstract metaphysics. The elder Hichens was also a talented musician, and Robert declined the opportunity to go to Oxford in favor of the Royal College of Music.

Hichens's autobiography records that before making this choice he had fallen in love, but that his suit was rejected by the girl's father on the grounds that he had no prospects. He admits to having been deeply wounded by this, but asserts that he survived to fall in love several more times. It is noticeable, though, that he makes no further reference to these other occasions. He notes, sadly, that the girl never did marry. Neither did he; he accepted, in the fullness of time, the respectable status of "confirmed bachelor," although he took far less pride in it than Marie Corelli took in her own defiant celibacy.

While studying in London Hichens immersed himself in bohemian life, admitting that he came "under the fascination of the obscure, the doubtful, the difficult, the tragic." He also admitted becoming fascinated—from a proper distance—by the "night-birds" of Piccadilly: the cheap prostitutes who used the darkness of Green Park to complete their hasty transactions. This fascination, in which attraction mingled with repulsion, is elaborately displayed in his intense early novel *Flames* (1897). At some point, though, he abruptly decided to abandon his projected career in music, and he transferred to the London School of Journalism. He proved an apt student, eventually replacing George Bernard Shaw as the music critic of the *World*.

One of the exercises in freelance journalism which Hichens undertook in the early 1890s was a series of articles about the occultism which was very fashionable in London at that time, and he interviewed numerous spiritualists, faith healers, palmists, and other poseurs of a similar stripe. Most of them he condemned as charlatans, but he remained convinced throughout his life that there was some essential truth underlying their various theories and supposed skills.

An important turning-point in Hichens's life—perhaps *the* important turning-point—was a trip to Egypt which he undertook in 1893-94, where he first made the acquaintance of the Sahara desert, and formed the impressions which were to be extrapolated so extravagantly in *The Garden of Allah*. A similar sense of the supernatural is even more extravagantly displayed in his novel *An Imaginative Man* (1895), which is explicitly based on his own exploits in Egypt.

Among the people Hichens met in Egypt was E. F. Benson, one of the sons of Archbishop Benson, who had just created a mild scandal by publishing a comic *roman à clef* about London High Society, *Dodo* (1893). *Dodo* was to be the prelude to a long and successful literary career, whose echoes extend to the present day in TV dramatizations of Benson's comic tales of Mrs. Mapp and "Lucia." Like Hichens, Benson also went on to write a good deal of supernatural fiction, and he too never married. At the same time, Hichens made the acquaintance of Lord Alfred Douglas, in whose company he travelled up the Nile.

Hichens's autobiography speaks of Lord Alfred in scrupulously polite and friendly terms, but—as one would expect—has nothing at all to say about his sexual proclivities. After their return to England, Lord Alfred introduced Hichens to Oscar Wilde, and Hichens's brief association with Wilde's circle, which was soon cut short by the famous trials, is reflected in the Dodoesque satire *The Green Carnation* (1894), which he published anonymously, only later confessing to Wilde that he was its author. Neither Wilde nor Douglas—according to Hichens, at least—was offended to find himself parodied in the novel, but the text had the perhaps fortunate effect, once its authorship was publicly acknowledged, of distancing Hichens in the public eye from the short-lived and ill-fated English Decadent movement.

\* \* \* \* \* \* \*

The peculiar influence of the journey up the Nile which Hichens took with Lord Alfred Douglas was elaborately displayed in much of his subsequent fiction before finally culminating in *The Garden of Allah*. The plot of *An Imaginative Man* is particularly interesting in this respect. Its protagonist is on honeymoon in Egypt, but under the spell of the wondrous environment he quickly falls out of love with his wife, and becomes fascinated instead by a tubercular young man who is attempting to drink his fill of life in the local vice dens before his inevitable demise. In the end, the protagonist abandons his wife in favor of an obsessive attachment to the Sphinx.

The Sphinx is, of course, the subject of Oscar Wilde's most famous poem, in which it becomes—among other things—a symbol of a syncretic exotic religiosity not so very far removed from that which seizes hold of Domini Enfilden. Another early story by Hichens dealing with the mesmeric fascination of North Africa, "The Charmer of Snakes" (in *Bye-Ways*, 1897), also features a ruined honeymoon, in which a bride lured away from her husband by the eponymous magician undergoes an apparent metamorphosis into a huge white snake.

A Wildean influence is clearly evident in *Flames*, which is the story of two young men who are fast friends despite their considerable differences in temperament. One of them, Valentine Cresswell, is possessed of a remarkable beauty and an effortless moral purity. The authority of Valentine's example enables his friend, Julian Addison, to resist the temptations of the flesh, as symbolized by the night-birds of Piccadilly, but Valentine is profoundly dissatisfied with his inability to feel the seductive force of vice, and he persuades Julian to join him in séances aimed at a partial exchange of personalities. Alas, Valentine's soul is dispossessed by that of an evil occultist named Marr, and his moral authority over his friend becomes malign. Julian is eventually saved from total moral and physical degradation only by the determined self-sacrifice of a golden-hearted tart named Cuckoo Bright.

*Flames* is, in one sense, Hichens's attempt to copy *The Picture of Dorian Gray*. It betrays a great deal more moral confusion than Wilde's perversely neat allegory, but its depth of feeling is unmistakable. It also strives hard for genuine philosophical depth; like many other *fin de siècle* novels it claims to have derived its metaphysics from Schopenhauer, and exhibits a certain familiarity with the work of the British popularizers of Nietzsche (who included the novelist John Davidson and the psychologist and literary critic Havelock Ellis). All this research must have paved the way for the more pretentious and idiosyncratic metaphysical speculations of *The Garden of Allah*.

A similar depth of tortuous feeling is exhibited by a remarkable group of short stories written immediately before and after *Flames*, which were collected under the apt and revealing title *Tongues of Conscience* (1900). One of these stories, "The Cry of the Child," had spoiled the friendship between Hichens and the editor of *The Pall Mall Magazine*, Lord Frederick Hamilton, because Hamilton had judged it too repulsive to be published. It is the story of a man haunted by the crying of a ghostly child which only he can hear: a supernatural or hallucinatory reminder of the fact that he once allowed a child of his own to die of neglect. His guilt-feelings drive him, perversely, to maltreat his second wife, whose eventual death in childbirth is represented as the provision of a heaven-sent opportunity for his redemption. Another item in the collection is the story for which Hichens is nowadays best remembered, thanks to its constant reprinting in exemplary anthologies of horror stories: "How Love Came to Professor Guildea."

"How Love Came to Professor Guildea" is elaborately expanded from a story initially published in *Pearson's Magazine* as "The Man Who Was Beloved." The sceptical scientist of the title boasts to the priest who is his only friend that he has conclusively put aside sympathy and sentimentality, and has no use for affection. The priest (whose own celibacy is far less pretentious) then witnesses his friend's decline into madness while he is haunted by a moronic spirit which dotes on him. Neither of the two men can see the ghost, but its presence and nature are weirdly confirmed by the professor's pet parrot, which begins to mimic "her" loathsomely loving gestures.

Animals which reflect the personalities of the dead in more commonplace fashion, thus becoming scourges of conscience and agents of revenge after the fashion of Edgar Allan Poe's "The Black Cat," feature in several other early Hichens stories, including "A Reincarnation" (1895; reprinted as "The Return of the Soul" in *The Folly of Eustace and Other Stories*, 1896), and the title-story of *The Black Spaniel and Other Stories* (1905). Another motif to which he returned again and again is the personality-transfer subplot of *Flames*, which recurs in *The Dweller on the Threshold* (1911), "The Sin of Envy" (1934), and the partly-autobiographical title story of *The Man in the Mirror*. Although the later texts are as dispirited as the rest of his later works, they do testify to Hichens continual fascination with themes involving "alternative selves": dark *doppelgängers* which embody the threat of moral degradation and physical debilitation.

Contemplation of these patterns in Hichens's work strongly suggests that his trip up the Nile was for him the culmination of some personal crisis, in which his own disturbed feelings were projected on to a wonderfully receptive landscape. Whether anything of significance occurred between Lord Alfred Douglas and Hichens we cannot know, but if one reads between the lines of both the resultant fiction and his autobiography. one is strongly encouraged to conclude that Hichens came to believe (as a well-brought-up Victorian easily might) that a commitment to celibacy was the appropriate answer to all his covert desires and inclinations, and that he stuck to this decision even though it proved difficult.

Whatever the temptations were whose awesome and awkward force is so obsessively reflected in Hichens's early works, writing *The Garden of Allah* does seem to have laid them to rest. The tranquillity of heart which Domini Enfilden eventually achieves through her reconciliation with the mysterious power of the desert seems to have been echoed in her creator's own being.

In one of the more striking of his later novels, *Dr Artz* (1929), Hichens (who was then sixty-five years old) contemplates with utter horror the exploits of a scientist based on the notorious Serge Voronoff, who proposed that virility might be restored to old men by transplanting the testicles of monkeys into their bodies to boost their testosterone levels. Hichens was apparently profoundly glad to have cut himself off from all the demands of sexuality and sentimentality—and he was presumably grateful that, unlike Professor Guildea, he was not to be hounded to the grave by the hauntings of idiotic lovesickness.

\* \* \* \* \* \* \*

This tentative explanation of the deep significance which *The Garden of Allah* had for its author leaves unanswered the question of why it proved so very popular. Indeed, the suggestion that it answered such an intimate personal need makes its wide commercial appeal seem even more puzzling. The fact that it reproduces the standard template of so many formularized love stories hardly helps, given that it stubbornly refuses to conclude with the climactic affirmation of the power of true love which is ritualized by such fiction, insisting instead on proceeding to the dissolution of the union thus produced. On the other hand, it must be noted that tragic variants of the standard formulaic romance were later to become popular in Hollywood. *The Garden of Allah* was filmed in 1936, an early adventure in Technicolor, with Marlene Dietrich as Domini and Charles Boyer—the star of several other notable tearjerkers—as Androvsky.

Perhaps the real point at issue here is that however bizarre and unlikely *The Garden of Allah* might be in matters of specific detail, it is essentially a novel about seeking and eventually finding a special kind of inner peace. In rejecting the common narrative hypothesis that such contentment can be found in marriage to one's soul-mate, it merely confirms the common experience of the majority; and in retaining the optimism that a relationship with a child might be more rewarding, it confirms the hope which most commonly triumphs over that experience.

In making these moves, *The Garden of Allah* must have seemed to many of its readers to be "more realistic" than more conventionally-reassuring fantasies, and thus to be a "real novel" with something valuable to say. This is, of course, all illusion, but nothing sells better in the marketplace of popular fiction (or, for that matter, the marketplace of popular nonfiction) than a compelling illusion.

Such was Robert Hichens's own depth of feeling that *The Garden of Allah* is utterly unashamed in luridly exaggerating the unease which spurs its central character onwards, ennobling and dignifying that unease by representing it as a desperate quest for spiritual enlightenment. The novel's vocabulary of ideas must have been entirely new to almost all its readers, and all the more striking by virtue of its novelty, but the feeling of personal unease which it transfigured so dramatically was as commonplace then as it is now.

Modern readers would have great difficulty in accepting the Sahara desert as a symbol and earthly embodiment of Purgatory, and would have even greater difficulty swallowing the tale of a renegade Trappist fleeing with the secret formula of a unique liqueur. But modern guides to "finding oneself" and modern recipes for contentment—whether offered in best-selling fiction or in best-selling nonfiction—only seem to be more plausible because their fancy dress carries the same gloss of apparent daring and originality that *The Garden of Allah* once carried. By the same token, any actual effect they have on their readers must in the final analysis be credited to the placebo effect. There are, after all, no true answers; there are only bearable compromises.

Robert Hichens seems to have found a compromise which was, for him, bearable; that is cause for congratulation no matter what one may think of the general suitability of his particular compromise. His achievement was all the more remarkable because the road which led him there seems, on the evidence of his work, to have been hard to travel because it was haunted by seductive and menacing phantoms and liberally strewn with sharp thorns and hidden pitfalls.

Because we all find our paths through life problematic, we should all be able to sympathize with a man who finds his to be bitterly vexatious, and should sympathize even with his most bizarre dramatizations of his predicament. Few of us would care to end up in the same situation as Domini Enfilden, but if the only alternative were to end up like Professor Guildea, we would take it and be glad. We ought, therefore, to understand—as the reading public of 1904 was evidently glad to do—why Domini was fully entitled to believe that her personal pilgrimage through purgatory had ultimately brought her to her true destiny.

# X.

# *I, CLAUDIUS*

 *I, Claudius* was published in 1934, exactly a hundred years after Edward Bulwer-Lytton's pioneering English novel of Roman decadence, *The Last Days of Pompeii*. It went through six editions between May and December and a further seven (the last four in a cheaper format) before the outbreak of World War II. The second part of the story, *Claudius the God and His Wife Messalina*, was issued six months after the first, in a much larger edition, which similarly had to be reprinted several times before going into a cheaper format. Because the two books are halves of a single literary entity, I shall feel free to use the title *I, Claudius* to refer to the whole as well as the part.

 Had it not been for wartime paper shortages, the two parts of *I, Claudius* might well have repeated their runaway success when they were released (in four volumes) as Penguin books in 1941, but circumstances ruled that their sales would be limited on the supply side. There is perhaps a certain irony in this, given that the cynical world-view of the books derives in large part from Graves's experiences in World War I. After the war, though, the books remained constantly in print, and their popularity was given a further boost in the 1970s when they were dramatized for BBC TV; the resultant serial remains one of the most spectacular highlights of British television history.

 There had never been a historical novel like *I, Claudius* before, and no subsequent attempt to employ its method has been anywhere near as successful. To seize upon a central figure in the rich tapestry of historical melodrama and to imagine him the writer of a frank and secret history of his own life and times required great panache on the part of the author, and once it had been done future exercises in the same vein could only rank as essays in imitation. In addition, Graves had plucked the best fruit from the tree; the central character he had chosen was uniquely useful in providing a view both long and broad of a uniquely fascinating period in history. Many men have lived through interesting times, but no one else was ever so close for so long to the political heart of such very interesting times as Claudius.

 The achievements of *I, Claudius* do not depend on conventional novelistic values. The narrative, for all its frankness, is mock-historical in both style and content. It is not much concerned with characterization, nor with the emotional life of its characters, nor even with the agonies of their personal dilemmas. It declines to exploit in any conspicuously lascivious manner the more lurid aspects of the careers of Caligula and Messalina. The main interest of both narrator and author is in the grand sweep of history, in political cause and consequence, and in the moral state of the world as a whole. A note in the Penguin edition of *Claudius the God* says that "it is history disguised as fiction rather than the other way about," and it is easy to see how one could make this mistake, given the extremely scrupulous research which went into the book and the way it is laid out. The truth is, however, that it is very much "the other way about." *I, Claudius* and its companion are fantasies on a grand scale. The cunning effect of their double disguise as history and sworn testimony is to add a powerful persuasive power to the fantasy. So much of what is related in the text is true that it is difficult for the reader to notice that what has been added to the truth is in fact a cunning pattern of outrageous inventions; but when one does observe that, one immediately realizes that these are inventions of a truly awesome magnitude and ambition.

\* \* \* \* \* \* \*

As everyone who saw the TV serial will readily remember, the true central character of the first part of *I, Claudius* is Livia, the wife of Augustus (who was brilliantly brought to life by Sian Phillips). She is recruited by Graves to be the mastermind planning and shaping the history of the Roman Empire from 38 B.C. to the accession of Nero in 54 A.D. (long after her death). Her instruments of determination are the careful management of information and the covert administration of poison; by these means she procures the banishment, execution, or murder of everyone who might disrupt her schemes. The purpose of those schemes—which belong, of course, entirely to Graves rather than to the historical Livia—is to ensure that the empire will pass into the unfortunate custody of her own son Tiberius rather than to any of the more apparent heirs who stand in his way.

The superficial motives which Graves credits to Livia in order to fit her for this Machiavellian role are a combination of straightforward nepotism and an ideological conviction that the empire must remain an empire rather than reverting to its republican roots. She thus appears villainous on two distinct counts: firstly because several of the potential heirs she removes seem much worthier men than the morose, perverse, and malevolent Tiberius; and secondly because the sympathies of the author, the narrator, and (this is taken for granted) the reader are all solidly anti-tyrannical, and hence, in this context, pro-republican.

Beneath this surface, however, the matter is by no means so simple. Claudius is at pains to point out that Livia, whatever her faults, is an administrator of genius, who runs the business side of the empire very well—far better, in fact, than Augustus or Tiberius could ever have done unaided. By means of such insistences, her Machiavellianism is at least partly excused. More importantly, a deeper level of motivation is provided in the form of a "secret" sibylline prophecy which Livia has, and evidently trusts—and which she ultimately surrenders to Claudius's custody, partly by way of explanation for her actions and partly in order that he too might become, in his turn, its conscious instrument.

This invented prophecy is a fascinating literary device. It is easy enough for the author of a historical novel to draft accurate "prophecies" and drop them into his plot at strategic moments, but there is far more involved in this particular instance than a mere tongue-in-cheek literary flourish. By making the "true" prophecy a significant covert cause of the events which he is interpreting, Graves transforms the whole meaning of those events.

From the point of view of the author and reader, Claudius the character is, of course, a prisoner of history. The events of his life are fixed by the historical record. The introduction of the prophecy, however, serves to make him in the end a conscious prisoner of history, whose principal reason for doing what he does in the latter stages of his life is to ensure that history will, in fact, work out the way we know it did. Thus, like Livia before him, he becomes an agent of a mysterious Fate, acting in defiance of his own sense of justice and propriety in order to ensure that he is succeeded by the vile Nero.

While he is contriving this disaster, Claudius is forced to excuse himself to the reader on the grounds that some more remote good might come of temporary evil, but in this he is doubly betrayed by his creator. Graves and the reader know perfectly well that the imaginary Fate which is supposedly "speaking" through the invented oracle has not the slightest intention of using Nero as a last straw to make the Roman people so sick of emperors that they will restore the republic. Claudius has been taken for a ride, and the "future" which faces the Roman world as he approaches his death is, in fact, far worse than he is permitted to imagine.

The particular prophecy which concludes chapter I of *I, Claudius* and the various other "true" omens which feature there and elsewhere in the plot do not seem out of place in the story, because we know full well that the Romans were obsessed with such divinations and omens. In purely rational terms, though, they are utterly inappropriate, because the first and foremost thing we know about prophecies and omens is how unreliable they are. Whatever the true motives of the historical Livia and Claudius may have been, the one thing of which we can be quite certain is that they did not arise from the possession of prophetic knowledge which was both true and known by them to be true.

As speculative history, therefore, Graves's story is a non-starter. If Livia was a poisoner at all she was certainly not a poisoner for the reasons cited in *I, Claudius*; and if Claudius really did do his best to ensure that Nero succeeded him, he certainly did not do it for the reasons cited in *Claudius the God*. But this does not mean that the novel is incompetent as a work of fiction; it merely means that if we want to understand what kind of fiction it is, then we must look more deeply into Graves's method and the circumstances which shaped the book.

Graves's own awareness of the paradoxicality of his work is amply displayed in chapter IX, which deals with the person Claudius calls—with heavily ironic significance—"the Last of the Romans": the historian Pollio. This passage describes how Claudius becomes the arbiter in a dispute between Pollio and Livy as to which of them writes history in the proper manner. Pollio is a scrupulous marshaller of facts who values minute accuracy above all else, while Livy makes a story out of history, recklessly imputing improbably modern motives to the men of the distant past in order to draw moral lessons from their fates. Graves's Claudius is very adamant in his preference for Pollio, but this serves only to emphasize the fact that Graves is working wholly (and ironically) in the tradition of Livy. *I, Claudius* is indeed a clever morality play which takes any and all convenient liberties to make its point, while disingenuously claiming all the while to be mere reportage.

\* \* \* \* \* \* \*

*I, Claudius* is essentially a book about civilization, and the attempt to preserve civilized values in a world which is threatened both from without and from within. The external threat is that of the unruly barbarians against whose marauding spirit firm borders must be maintained. The internal threat is a rottenness at the imperial core: the absolute corruption which, according to Lord Acton, inevitably comes in the train of absolute power. From the viewpoint of Claudius, of course, it is the latter threat which is the greater, and the external menace only becomes powerful when and because the weakness induced by internal corruption permits it.

Graves was, of course, as keenly aware as his predecessor Bulwer-Lytton of the parallels which were frequently drawn in the political rhetoric of Westminster between the Roman Empire and the British Empire. He fully appreciated the ironic scepticism which extended the metaphor to find a pre-destined decline and fall of the British Empire by virtue of the same faults that had brought the Roman Empire to decadence and destruction. He was perfectly willing to draw such parallels himself in poems (written after *I, Claudius*) such as "The Fallen Tower of Siloam" and "The Cuirassiers of the Frontier." Like so many of his generation, his original optimistic view of such matters had been shattered and completely overturned by his experiences as an officer in the Great War, which had been advertised as a "war to save civilization," and had turned out to be something very different.

Graves first made his reputation as a war poet. He survived the Somme but was severely wounded thereafter. Ironically, he probably owed his survival to the severity of the wounds, whose effects were compounded by his premature return to the front—a return that soon occasioned a relapse which forced his permanent retirement from active service. His friend Siegfried Sassoon was not so lucky, and when Sassoon was threatened with a court-martial for refusing to return to action and speaking publicly against the war, Graves appeared as a witness on his behalf before a medical board. There he argued forcefully that Sassoon should be excused on the grounds of his mental ill-health, later recalling that he broke down in tears three times while giving his evidence. He became sharply aware of the paradoxicality of what he had done and said; the real truth of the matter, in his view, was that Sassoon was perfectly sane, while the men promulgating the war were quite mad.

Many of Graves's poems about the war were to put forward the proposition that the thoughtful fighting-men at the front were the only good and honest defenders of the values of civilization, and that those who sent them forth to die were worse than the men who actually killed them. In *I, Claudius*, the barbarians who continually threaten the borders of the empire are called, in no-nonsense fashion, Germans, but they are not the real enemy. The British are, of course, barbarians too until their cunning conqueror Claudius shows them the error of their ways; Claudius does not know, although the reader does, that this domestication is a strictly temporary affair whose rewards will be lost during the forthcoming Dark Ages.

Claudius also does not know, of course, that the wreckage of the empire which he leaves to Nero will eventually fall into the hands of the Christians. As it had for Bulwer-Lytton a hundred years before, the issue of Christianity posed certain diplomatic problems for Graves, but the risks he ran were far less. Bulwer-Lytton never could bring himself explicitly to embrace the pagan naturalism which he credited to his villain Arbaces, no matter how strongly he felt its attraction, but Graves had not the stern force of Victorian censorship to intimidate him. Graves felt free to despise such carefully devout examples of historical fiction as Lew Wallace's *Ben-Hur* (1880) and Henryk Sienkiewicz's *Quo Vadis?* (1896), and equally free to appreciate the clever scepticism of Anatole France's *The White Stone* (1905), in which a group of exiled Roman intellectuals can find nothing to admire in St. Paul while readily attaching their hopes for the salvation of civilization to Nero.

The orthodox religious faith which Graves had once possessed had been annihilated by the war, and he seized the opportunity which *I, Claudius* gave him to indulge the fervor of his conversion. He took the trouble to include in his preface to *Claudius to God* a dutiful, quasi-apologetic note to the effect that Claudius's hostility to Christianity is an unavoidable matter of historical record, but his own voice clearly echoes in the sour tones of some of Claudius's scathing comments. Interestingly, the would-be Messiah who is very extensively featured in Claudius's account of the years of his reign is not Jesus but Herod Agrippa, who comes to the brink of establishing his own empire in the East, centred upon Jerusalem. He is thwarted at the last by the intervention—which seems to be explicitly supernatural—of that same Fate which is patiently guiding Rome to disaster.

In these ways, the actions and opinions of Claudius continually reflect—obliquely, but pertinently—upon the condition of modern England. Claudius's vague and ultimately hopeless dreams of a return to the days of republican democracy are thus metaphorically transformed into a deep pessimism regarding the fate of England. The nation is viewed as if it were struggling hopelessly under the burden of a senseless and ultimately destructive destiny. It is probably significant that while Graves wrote *I, Claudius* he was living in virtual exile in Majorca with the poet Laura Riding, who had an enormous influence on his work and for whom he had deserted his first wife. His personal feelings of alienation must have been easily transformed in his imagination into a much more grandiose dissatisfaction with the perennially sick state of the realm from which he had become a shell-shocked refugee.

\* \* \* \* \* \* \*

Graves always represented *I, Claudius*—and, indeed, all of his prose—as hackwork; in his own view he was primarily a poet and it was by his poetry alone that he desired his literary worth to be judged. Hackwork or not, though, one can find in *I, Claudius* the seeds of a series of preoccupations which came increasingly to the fore in all Graves's later work. Not only were its ideas about the unease of empires to find more earnest redeployment in his poetry, but its sceptical accounts of the origins of Christianity were to be much elaborated in his carefully-researched but calculatedly heretical novel *King Jesus* (1946). The most significant continuing thread was, however, the extraordinary elaboration of the novel's method which ultimately produced the extended essay on myth, *The White Goddess* (1947).

*The White Goddess* is a monumental work of calculated pseudo-scholarship which annoys many of its academic readers because some non-academic readers take what it says at face value, treating it as if it were a serious study in anthropology. Any authentic anthropologist can easily produce dozens of facts and arguments to demonstrate that its accounts of the nature, evolution, and meaning of the myths with which it deals are entirely false, but the book should not be regarded either as a catalogue of mistakes or as a hoax. It is a fantasy, in exactly the same way that *I, Claudius*, for all its sly protestations to be history, is a fantasy, and it is similarly a fantasy with a purpose. Like Margaret Murray's amazing work of pseudo-scholarship, *The Witch-Cult in Western Europe* (1921)—which really does seem to have been a patchwork of self-delusions—it borrows very heavily from the great classic of twentieth-century scholarly fantasy, James Frazer's *The Golden Bough* (1890-1915), but it is difficult to believe that a researcher as scrupulous as Graves could ever have taken Frazer's soaring flights of the imagination for fact or reputable theory; it is far more likely that he understood perfectly well what fabulous creativity there was in Frazer's endeavor, thought it a worthwhile poetic enterprise, and therefore set out to outdo his model.

What *The White Goddess* does, in a sense, is to put a face upon that mysterious Fate which, as the issuer of true prophecies and sender of accurate omens, becomes the prime mover of the history laid out in *I, Claudius* and *Claudius the God*. Simply put, the thesis of the book is that the authentic Muse of all true poets is identifiable with a series of pagan goddesses associated with the moon, who reigned supreme in a hypothetical prehistoric age when human societies were Matriarchally-organized and ecologically virtuous. Graves identifies the Celtic goddess Cerridwen as an archetype of the species, and makes much of the rites of (male) human sacrifice supposedly associated with her worship. Graves was not the first British poet to develop such an eccentric fascination with pagan goddesses—John Cowper Powys's monumental novel *A Glastonbury Romance* (1932) concludes with a long and curious hymn to Cybele—but no one else had ever taken the trouble to formalize his ideas in a scholarly fantasy like *The White Goddess*.

The account of early British mythology which forms the core of *The White Goddess* is uninhibitedly elaborated from the post-Frazerian anthropological fantasies of Lewis Spence, whose ideas are also echoed in the lurid account of the Druid religion which Claudius offers in chapter XVI of *Claudius the God*; but there are more subtle ways in which *I, Claudius* foreshadows the later book, including Claudius's reverent attitude to the women who play the role of sibyl, and Graves's curiously ambivalent attitude to the character of Livia.

In terms of virtue, *I, Claudius* is as misogynistic as it is misanthropic; the only good woman in the entire story (indeed, the only authentically virtuous person, although excuses are made for a handful of honest warriors whose violence and cruelty are purely matters of duty) is the provident whore Calpurnia. In terms of the efficient exercise of power, however, the women win hands down; they have a virtual monopoly on capability. The men who are the ostensible rulers are consistently duped and manipulated by their womenfolk; even mad Caligula is besotted with his sisters and ultimately captivated, to the extent that his wayward spirit can be captivated, by the deceptive

Caesonia. The principal exception to the generalization is the near-messiah Herod Agrippa; Emperor Claudius at the height of his power, with Livia behind him, Messalina to the right and Calpurnia to the left, and Agrippinilla awaiting him, is the most hag-ridden of them all. Thus, the Fate which employs Livia as its instrument is female through and through; part of its mechanism is to force Livia to preserve Claudius by persuading her that her hopes of becoming a goddess herself depend on his accession to the throne (and so, it inevitably transpires, they do).

The unusual role which Laura Riding played in Graves's life is certainly not irrelevant to this developing obsession, but should not be overestimated, and might easily be reckoned a symptom rather than a cause. It is probably more appropriate to see Graves's formulation of this new and idiosyncratic mythology in terms of a series of inversions by which he reacted against, rejected, and comprehensively overturned the thoroughly masculine values which had been so carefully inculcated in him by his education at Charterhouse and in the Welsh Fusiliers. It is notable that his revisionist account of *King Jesus* produces a far more militaristic and worldly ambitious figure than the orthodox view. Jesus here becomes, in fact, far more like the Herod Agrippa of *Claudius the God* than the spiritually-inclined figurehead of modern Christianity. Significantly, though, the text also makes Jesus the partner and instrument of a whole series of Marys, who are collectively offered as the appropriate object of a revisionist Mariolatry.

\* \* \* \* \* \* \*

It is worth bearing in mind, in considering historical novels in general and *I, Claudius* in particular, that all history involves a measure of fantasy. Historical understanding is essentially an understanding of the motives of the actors involved, but those motives can only be reconstructed by an act of the imagination which involves "putting ourselves in their shoes." We may be greatly assisted in so doing by a knowledge of the facts of history—the impersonal record of what happened and when—and by the writings of the actors and those who knew them, but experience teaches us to be very wary of the accounts which people offer of their own motives and the motives of their associates. We know only too well what a strong interest people have in overlaying accounts of why they did what they did with excuses and rationalizations, and we readily appreciate why the historian in search of a proper understanding always has to read between the lines of the records available to him instead of taking them at face value.

A scrupulous academic historian, like Claudius's hero Pollio, always tries to keep this fantasy to a minimum, and is content to leave a substantial margin of uncertainty in his understanding. There are others, however—like Livy and Graves—for whom this margin of uncertainty becomes a exploitable opportunity: a space for constructive fantasization. For "creative historians" of this kind, the past may be reconstructed in the interests of the present, made into a fable or a parable for the purposes of moral instruction. The writer of this stripe who exploits his poetic license to the full—as Graves does by inserting an inverted hindsight into his story to operate as a dour destiny—may complete the circle of his argument by reimporting that sense of predestined doom into his interpretation of the modern world, where it may become an "explanation" of a sense of helplessness in the face of a hostile and implacable Fate.

It is not surprising that Graves was eventually to write a "prophecy" of his own in his Utopian novel *Seven Days in New Crete* (1949; known in the U.S. as *Watch the Northwind Rise*), in which the imaginary past of *The White Goddess* is reconstructed as a hypothetical future. Like all real prophecies—and quite unlike the ones which are deployed in *I, Claudius*—this fantasy has not an atom of genuine foresight in it, and even its hopes are far too idiosyncratic to be shared by anyone but its author and a handful of devoted admirers.

As Pollio points out, the kind of fantasized reportage in which men like Graves indulge is not good history, but fantasy has ends of its own which are not to be despised. Mental life involves a very substantial component of fantasy, and it is by no means obvious that success in mental life benefits from the reduction of that fantasy to a minimum. Indeed, there are good grounds for thinking that success in many kinds of everyday endeavors may be increased by the careful deployment of the various kinds of enthusiastic fantasy which may be grouped under the heading of "positive thinking."

We all use fantasy as a means of adapting to the world in which we find ourselves, and there are probably very few of us who could not benefit from a cleverer exploitation of its resources. Robert Graves began in *I, Claudius* a series of exploitative moves which ultimately led him into imaginative territory which was frankly bizarre, but he was urged on by the pressure of terrible and extraordinary experiences. Given this, his long odyssey through the territories which lie on the mythical borderlands of history can be recognized as an authentically heroic endeavor as well as an understandable one.

# PART THREE

# PASSING JUDGMENT:

# ASSORTED CRIMES AND PUNISHMENTS

# XI.

# *THE MYSTERIES OF PARIS*

The author of *The Mysteries of Paris*, Eugène Sue, was born in 1804. His father and grandfather were medical men of some distinction, and he was initially intended to follow in their footsteps. After completing his education he served for a while as a ship's doctor, but preferred to work as a journalist and a writer of colorful melodramas. He wrote prolifically, achieving moderate success with his early tales of the sea, including the novella *Atar-Gull* (1831; translated as *Atar-Gull; or, The Slave's Revenge* and as *The Negro's Revenge; or, Brulart the Black Pirate*) and the novel *La Vigie de Koat-Vën* (1833; translated as *The Temptation; or, The Watch-Tower of Koat-Vën.*

Having inherited his father's money, Sue set himself up as a Parisian man-about-town, in which capacity his luxurious tastes and flamboyant dandyism soon made him a living legend. In 1834 he became a founder member of the French Jockey Club, and wrote a history of the Godolphin Arabian (one of the stallions from which all racing thoroughbreds descend). Not unnaturally, he soon began to produce novels set in the world of Parisian high society, including *Arthur* (1838) and *Mathilde, mémoires d'une jeune femme* (1841). These exhibited his growing interest in social reform and gave voice to some marginally Radical ideals. In the meantime, he continued to produce wilder romances, most notably *Lautréamont* (1838)—a historical novel set in the days of Louis XIV, whose title was borrowed as a pseudonym by the author of the infamous *Les Chants du Maldoror* (1868)—and *Le Morne-au-diable* (1842; translated as *The Female Bluebeard* and as *The Refugees of Martinique*), which offered an extravagant account of the exploits of a female pirate.

It is probable that Sue's society novels were influenced by the early society novels of Sue's English contemporary, Edward Bulwer-Lytton, and Bulwer-Lytton's experiments in early crime fiction may also have helped to inspire the direction which Sue's work subsequently took. Whereas Bulwer-Lytton was eventually rehabilitated to the comfortable security of the English aristocracy, however, Sue became increasingly absorbed in Radical ideas. Although Bulwer-Lytton was eventually made into the most successful of nineteenth-century English writers by reprints of his works issued as cheap "railway novels," he had to produce them in the first instance for publication as three-deckers aimed at the relatively well-off patrons of the circulating libraries. Had Sue continued to be constrained by circumstance to slant his own work to such a market, his career would doubtless have been very different, but in fact he found an opportunity to publish in a new medium for a much wider audience, and thus became one of the first writers ever to obtain an audience which extended into the lower strata of a society still marked by extreme class divisions.

One of the legacies of the Revolution of 1789 was that the movement towards universal literacy proceeded more rapidly in France than anywhere else. The post-Revolutionary French also shared with the post-Revolutionary Americans the notion that a healthy press was a vital cornerstone of a free and just society. In Britain the freedom of the press was restricted by taxation, particularly by stamp duty, which made newspapers artificially expensive and forced them to forge strong and intimate links with the interests of a bourgeois audience. Advertisements were also taxed, compounding the disincentive to manufacturers of ordinary consumer goods to hawk their wares through newspaper advertising. In France, by contrast, the demand for reading material created by the spread of literacy offered an opportunity for the proprietors of newspapers—aided and abetted by advertisers—to provide a product of universal appeal. There quickly developed a circulation war among French daily papers, and one of the weapons with which that war was fought was *le roman feuilleton*: a serial novel whose melodramatic thrust was calculated to be sufficiently engaging to make readers anxious to acquire every episode.

*Le Siècle* launched the first *roman feuilleton* in 1836, but it was not until the early 1840s that the experiment had proved its worth. It was then that editors began to compete fiercely to secure the services of authors who could adapt their working methods to the rigorous regime of producing daily episodes of a story which—if it proved popular enough—might be extended over many months. Balzac and George Sand were among those who tried their hands at the new craft, but a rigorous regime of natural selection soon exposed the two men who emerged as its supreme practitioners, and hence became the two most popular writers in French literary history: Sue was one and Alexandre Dumas was the other. The breakthrough work, which fully demonstrated the potential of this curious new medium, was Sue's *Les Mystères de Paris*, which ran in *Le Journal des Débats* from 19 June 1842 to 15 October 1843.

\* \* \* \* \* \* \*

The newspaper editors of Paris had quickly discovered the remarkable truth which is responsible for the seemingly paradoxical face

of modern journalism: the vast majority of potential newspaper readers
are not really interested in news which is of real political and economic
significance; they prefer "human interest stories," and what they like
best of all is to read of matters sensational and scandalous, especially
when these have a local connection of some kind, or when they involve
royalty. Sue imported these "news values" into his fiction with great
enthusiasm.

The plot of *The Mysteries of Paris* is firmly located in the
streets, the prisons, the hospitals, and the asylums of Paris. It features
a host of abominable villains whose vileness knows no limits, who col-
laborate with the cruel blows inflicted by ill-fortune and bad laws upon
a veritable legion of virtuous working folk. The desperate attempts
made by these humble but virtuous individuals to get by in life are continually aided by the charitable efforts of a paragon of princely nobility,
who habitually goes among them incognito (as many good princes of
legend have been implausibly rumored to do).

*The Mysteries of Paris* is, therefore, a novel of calculated extremes. Its multi-stranded story moves from drinking-dens and dun-
geons to grand houses and palaces, but binds all its scenes together with
a convoluted series of contrivances in which—by means of astonishingly far-reaching patterns of coincidence—everyone turns out to be
related by blood or by conspiracy to everyone else. No previous work
had ever offered to the poor such a sense of being part of the world, or
such wild fantasies of salvation from their most desperate plights, and
none had ever addressed the rich with such frankness on the subject of
the desperate plight of the poor and the practical possibilities of its alle-
viation.

Dumas was as shameless a melodramatist as Sue, but he
worked for papers which had a different political bias, and while Sue
became increasingly the Radical in his subsequent works, Dumas increasingly cultivated a kind of nostalgic Royalism. Sue followed *The
Mysteries of Paris* with another sprawling epic, *Le Juif errant* (*Le Constitutionnel*, 25 June 1844-12 July 1845; translated as *The Wandering
Jew*), which ran in direct competition with Dumas's two most celebrated works, *The Three Musketeers* and *The Count of Monte Cristo*.
While Dumas retreated into the realms of the glorifiable past and wish-
fulfillment fantasy, Sue—who had already demonstrated his own skill
in aristocratic historical romance in *Lautréamont*—chose to intensify his
crusade on behalf of the poor people of Paris.

In *The Wandering Jew* Sue's archvillains are the Jesuits and
their aristocratic supporters. The inevitable result of this was that Dumas secured the wholehearted approval of society, while Sue came to be
thought dangerous, nowhere more so than in England, where his works
were very rapidly translated for publication in cheap "penny dreadful"
formats. Sue was for a while the most popular writer in England, at
least among the lower orders, and he was extravagantly imitated by the

indefatigable G. W. M. Reynolds, founder of *Reynolds' Miscellany* and *Reynolds' News*, who made his own name as a dangerous Radical with *The Mysteries of London* (1846-48) and *The Mysteries of the Court of London* (1849-56). (There was, incidentally, a French *Mysteries of London* too, commissioned by *Le Courier Français* from the third most successful of the feuilletonists, Paul Féval, as a direct response to Sue.)

Ironically, Dumas's nostalgic regard for a past when chivalry always triumphed over chicanery and bad kings could be marvellously replaced by their virtuous twins never went out of date. Simplified translations of his works were considered appropriate fodder for a popular series of English "children's classics" even in the 1960s. Sue is much less well-known, and hardly read at all, although the English texts of *The Mysteries of Paris* and *The Wandering Jew* have both been recently reprinted by Dedalus. His vivid interest in the contemporary misfortunes of the Parisian poor seems to many readers to be of antiquarian interest only. It might be remembered, however, that it was the example of *The Mysteries of Paris* which inspired Victor Hugo to write *Les Misérables* (1862), and that the street-urchins who daily prance and warble their way across the stage of London's Palace Theatre in the long-running musical based on Hugo's story are in a direct line of descent from Sue's daily doses of sensationalism. The influence which Sue had on English popular fiction was very considerable, and although the tradition of Victorian melodrama which owed so much to him has now died out, we can still see echoes of his techniques in TV soap operas and "blockbuster" bestsellers.

\* \* \* \* \* \* \*

The central story-line of *The Mysteries of Paris* concerns a young girl named Fleur-de-Marie (Flower of the Virgin), also known as La Goualeuse (approximately, Sweet-Throat or Songstress). We first meet her working for an "ogress" who is a whoremistress and keeper of a drinking den. As the story begins she is being menaced by a lout nicknamed Le Chourineur (Slasher), whose rough demands that she spare him the price of a drink are interrupted by a mysterious stranger named Rodolphe. Rodolphe gives Le Chourineur a good hiding for threatening the girl, but then buys drinks for both of them, and listens to the stories of their wretched lives. He learns that they are essentially good-hearted folk who have been treated with abominable cruelty by those who had charge of them, and have had no chance to be other than what they are.

Rodolphe has ventured into the slums in disguise in the hope of tracing the address of a clerk named Germain, who is the long-lost son of a woman he has previously aided. He is in reality a wealthy German prince with the power and the will to aid worthy unfortunates, and he sets the plot of the novel in motion by his attempts to provide both La Goualeuse and Le Chourineur with new careers. The consequences of this generous impulse unfold over nearly half a million words, in a plot which gradually spreads out to take in and intricately entwine the fates of all those who have ever known La Goualeuse, whether as fast friends or deadly enemies. Her enemies become involved with the enemies of the Prince, as do the enemies of her friends.

Although it is by no means easy for the reader to keep track of all the entangled relationships which connect the elements of the plot, one all-important fact constantly maintains suspense: unknown to either of them until the climax, La Goualeuse is the beloved daughter whom Rodolphe has long thought dead. The reader discovers this at any early stage, but most of the various characters who have possession of the parts of the informational jigsaw have pressing reasons for keeping them secret, and the rest do not realize the significance of what they know. The fully-informed reader must therefore watch the characters slowly groping their way towards a proper understanding of the grand pattern. In the meantime, the innocent characters must suffer the consequence of their own and others' ignorance. In particular, the saintly but horribly unfortunate La Goualeuse is continually under threat of spoliation, vitriolization, and murder by those who wish her harm.

The villains of *The Mysteries of Paris* include several hideously nasty petty criminals, but the full force of the author's hatred is mostly reserved for the miserly notary, Jacques Ferrand, whose machinations are hidden behind a mask of respectability and piety. It is Ferrand who—in order to keep for himself the allowance given to him by her unworthy and uncaring mother—delivered La Goualeuse as an infant to be the slave and victim of the monstrous La Chouette (Screech-Owl), and now would like the evidence of his crime permanently put away. The girl's more immediate persecutors include a multiple murderer with a mutilated face known as Le Maître d'École (Schoolmaster), who is actually the father of Germain (although this fact is mercifully never revealed to anyone but himself and a gang of river-pirates).

In parallel with the exploits of these inhabitants of the Underworld, Sue chronicles the lives of the poor but decent inhabitants of a lodging-house. These include the oppressed family of a lapidary named Morel (who are also victims of Ferrand) and the happy seamstress Rigolette Dimpleton, a friend of Germain's who becomes a confidante and instrument of Rodolphe's after he takes care to cultivate her acquaintance on that count. The lodging-house also serves to introduce the principal aristocratic character, Clémence d'Harville, who has a murderess for a stepmother and has been inveigled into marriage with an epileptic (Sue, according to the unfortunate and entirely mistaken opinion of the day, considered epilepsy to be a horrible form of hereditary madness).

Clémence comes close to spoiling her own virtue in a rendezvous at the lodging-house, but is deflected and subsequently saved from dishonor by Rodolphe. Sue takes care to establish that the aristocracy is no more and no less divided in its virtue than the lowest class of all, harboring its full quota of malice and deceit. Evidence that the author had begun to repent his earlier lifestyle is provided in the character of the wastrel dandy Viscount Saint-Rémy, who betrays the example set by his moderate father and goes to the bad, ultimately resorting to forgery and theft to support his extravagance before being driven into exile.

\* \* \* \* \* \* \*

The real power of the plot of *The Mysteries of Paris* is generated by the way in which the villainous characters go to their destruction. The almost hysterical excess of these passages is quite remarkable, and it attracted much criticism as well as much enthusiasm. Le Maître d'École, captured early on in the plot by Rodolphe, is deliberately blinded by the prince as a punishment for his crimes, but the full horror of this fate only unfolds by slow degrees as he tries to carry forward his career of infamy regardless. When the two female river pirates go to the guillotine, Sue dwells on their anticipatory sensations at great length. A fate even more horrific than these is reserved for Ferrand. Mere death, in Sue, is never enough to repay the dastardly for their crimes; indeed, he regards death as a mercy better kept for the release of innocents too badly wounded by life to go on.

Such scenes as the deliberate blinding of Le Maître d'École and the eventual destruction of La Chouette led Sue's detractors to accuse him of sadism, but the charge is mistaken. What such scenes actually strive for is an appropriate expression of an outrage so profound that nothing but extremes of horror can possibly assuage it. There is a key passage in the novel set in La Force (the main prison of Paris at the time) in which a petty thief nicknamed Pique-Vinaigre (Sharp Vinegar) must unwittingly play Scheherazade, spinning out a story to frustrate the planned murder of the unjustly-imprisoned Germain. Pique-Vinaigre points out—presumably echoing the author's fascination with an equivalent discovery—that the thieves and murderers who constitute his audience love more than any others stories in which the victims of appalling cruelty are eventually released by virtue of circumstances which send their tormentors to extraordinarily dreadful fates. His fellow prisoners—understandably—have no time at all for stories in which criminals much like themselves end up beneath the guillotine, but they nevertheless retain a more profound sense of morality which gladly and greatly rejoices in the unusual punishment of the unusually wicked.

In this section of the narrative Sue takes leave to lecture his readers at some length on the inequities of the law and the penal system, and the necessity of their reform. The substance of his case is that many of the men who find themselves in prison are there because of irremediable misfortune, and that the principal effect of imprisonment is to make them more skilled criminals by association with others more hardened than themselves. In his plots Sue practises exactly what he preaches; he firmly distinguishes between those criminals who, like Le Chourineur, retain a certain essential "heart" and "honor" and those who give themselves over entirely to predatory cruelty; for the latter, whether or not they are delivered into the hands of the law, fates every bit as hideous as he can contrive are most carefully and fervently designed.

It was this practice, if anything, which made Sue authentically dangerous as a potential rabble-rouser; his political ideals and reformist programs were mostly moderate and by no means revolutionary, but his outrage—and the outrage of his readers, which he flattered and served so uncompromisingly—was something else. For him, the worst of crimes inflamed such indignation that nothing within the law would serve as recompense, and for him the worst crimes of all were crimes of greed and ambition masked by respectable appearances: the crimes of crooked lawyers, corrupt bailiffs, and poison-supplying doctors. The thought of that kind of indignation spreading through the lower orders was one to trouble the minds of all gentlefolk.

At the end of the day, however, Sue could not contrive a whole-hearted escape from the prison of contemporary morality, and he failed to carry through the bold thrust of his own ideals. The most curious, and in some ways the most gut-wrenching, of all the passages in *The Mysteries of Paris* is the concluding one, which takes place after all has finally been revealed. Rodolphe has not only been reunited with his daughter but has legitimated her by hurriedly marrying her mother. Death instantly carries off the unworthy mother, so that she may neither benefit from her long record of infamy nor prevent Rodolphe's eventual union with the providentially-widowed Clémence D'Harville, but this happy ending has a canker at its heart which then proceeds to eat it away.

Sue cannot ever bring himself to forget, or fully to forgive, that no matter how little choice she had in the matter, La Goualeuse had briefly been a whore—and because Sue cannot forget or forgive it, neither can she. That her true place in the world is that of a princess there is not a shadow of doubt, and her saintliness continues to increase when she belatedly comes into that inheritance—but her sense of guilt and shame poison her peace of mind, and in the end she is condemned by her creator (at the ripe old age of eighteen) to a death which some readers might consider every bit as frightful as the ultimate fate of Le Maître d'École. There is a perversity in this slow slaughter which exceeds the more conventional tear-jerking of Charles Dickens's long-drawn-out execution of Little Nell in *The Old Curiosity Shop* (1841), and might more appropriately be likened to Samuel Richardson's astonishingly languorous excruciation of the unluckily-ravaged Clarissa Harlowe in *Clarissa* (abridged edition, 1747-48; full text, 1749).

\* \* \* \* \* \* \*

In *The Wandering Jew*, too, Sue finds it impossible to contrive a conventional happy ending. Here many good-hearted characters are similarly persecuted, by virtue of being heirs to a huge fortune (although they do not know it. In the end most of them are destroyed without ever finding out why—and, in some cases, without ever realizing that they have been victims of villainy—but the fortune is withheld in the end even from those who survive, some of whom find themselves worse off financially than when they started. Sue's growing Socialist convictions regarding the nobility of honest labor and modest means presumably had much to do with the design of this ending, but as a climax to an extravagant romance it seems fatally pusillanimous. Even at the allegorical level the story's moral seems faint-hearted. *The Wandering Jew*—who plays no active part in the plot—is symbolic of the plight of the exploited artisan, while his female counterpart Herodias symbolizes the plight of oppressed womankind, but the long-awaited redemption which is ultimately handed down to them by the author is curiously ambiguous.

Because of the huge success of *The Mysteries of Paris*, several serial translations of *The Wandering Jew* into English began while the plot was still unfolding, but it is probable that the enthusiasm of its importers would not have been so great had they known in advance what the dénouement would be. Sue's subsequent works were far less well-received in England. His series of novellas, *Les Sept péchés capitaux* (1847-48), was also translated simultaneously—as *The Seven Deadly Sins*—by two English penny periodicals, but it was not widely reprinted and is now entirely forgotten, as is another penny-dreadful serial, *Martin the Foundling* (1848), which was a slightly belated translation of *Martin l'enfant trouvé, ou les mémoires d'un valet de chambre* (1846).

The English periodicals did not bother at all with the huge family saga *Les Mystères de peuple* (1849-52), a sprawling series of novellas and short novels which Sue considered to be his magnum opus, even though it unerringly selects out the most melodramatic episodes of history as stages for its long chronicle of outrageous misfortune. A translation of some early episodes was issued in England as *The Rival Races; or, The Sons of Joel* (1863), but was never augmented. *The Silver Cross; or, The Carpenter of Nazareth* may have been considered too controversial by virtue of its unrepentant invasion of sacred ground, although it was issued separately in the USA in 1899. A full translation of the work into English was finally made by the noted American socialist Daniel De Leon, whose New York Labor News Company issued its nineteen volumes (out of chronological order) as *The Mysteries of the People: The History of a Proletarian Family Across the Ages* between 1904 and 1911. Such units as *The Iron Collar; or, Faustina and Syomara* (1909), which displays the iniquities of Roman slavery and the horrors of the arena, and *The Iron Pincers; or, Mylio and Karvel* (1909), about the persecution of the Albigensian heretics, confirmed in the eyes of some commentators Sue's reputation for sadism. The historical accuracy of the work leaves as much to be desired as that of Dumas, but its ambitious scope remained unparalleled for many years and it provided a model for Henri Barbusse's time-spanning Socialist epic, *Les Enchaînements* (1925; translated as *Chains*) and Vardis Fisher's elaborately pretentious *Testament of Man* (12 volumes, 1943-60).

It was, perhaps, not entirely fortunate for Sue that his literary career extended through such interesting times. Had he not become a feuilletonist, his dalliance with Radical ideas might never have developed into the fierce interest in social reform which ultimately drew him to a species of Socialism derived from his reading of Proudhon. (Sue died in 1857, probably without ever having encountered the work of Karl Marx, although Marx was living in Paris in 1843-45, while *The Wandering Jew* was being serialized.) This fierce interest made Sue avidly enthusiastic to play a role when the revolution of 1848 began. Coincidentally, the Communist rising in Paris occurred on 15 May, the day after *Les Sept péchés capitaux* concluded its serialization in *Le Constitutionnel*. The new Republican constitution was promulgated in November, and in the following year Sue was elected a Socialist deputy for the Seine.

Unfortunately, the new constitution lasted only three years before the duly elected president, Louis Napoléon, abolished it in the wake of his *coup d'état*. Sue conscientiously opposed the coup, with the consequence that he was exiled from the city whose miseries and mysteries had moved him to such outrage, and he was never able to return to it. He went to Annecy in the Savoy (which was then independent of France), and that was where he died, no longer the spendthrift lover of luxury he once had been, nor even the best-selling writer he had so briefly and so spectacularly become. It was an ending as unsatisfactory, in its own way, as the endings of his most famous books.

# XII.

## *BEAU GESTE*

It is no easy task to explain—or even to explore—the awesome narrative force deployed by the author of *Beau Geste*, because P. C. Wren always did his very best to make a secret of himself. His entry in *Who's Who* was determinedly uninformative, revealing only that he had an M.A. from Oxford and offering a list of his novels. Of his parentage, family, and interests he carefully said nothing (although we know from the dedications in his books that he was married). His entry in *The Authors' and Writers' Who's Who* was similar, although the observation was added (possibly by the editor) that he had served in the English and Indian armies, and in the French Foreign Legion.

When Wren answered the questionnaire which Q. D. Leavis sent to contemporary writers while researching her book on *Fiction and the Reading Public* (1932), he took great care to deny that he was to be reckoned a professional novelist, and was vehemently insistent that he was not a "long-haired literary cove." The bulk of his readers, Wren opined, were the "cleanly-minded virile outdoor sort of people," and he was thankful that the particular publishers with whom he dealt had contrived to remain "sportsmen and gentlemen" even though they had "strayed into the muddy paths of commerce." His personal view of what made a bestseller was that such a book must contain "a searching appeal to the honest simple feelings and 'all that is best' in the great heart of the great public." His bookplate, autographed copies of which he often attached to books dispensed as gifts, displayed a coat of arms with the motto: *Virtuti Fortuna Comes*.

Wren might conceivably have believed wholeheartedly in his own straightforwardness, but the preoccupations of his fiction suggest strongly that it was a mere mask. All his central characters are ostensibly of the type and the faith which he claimed for his own, but every one of them is also the tormented victim of some hideously cruel circumstance of which pride will never allow him to speak. This cannot help but put an ironic and enigmatic gloss on Wren's stubborn silence about so many aspects of his own life.

\* \* \* \* \* \* \*

Percival Christopher Wren was born in 1885. If he ever did serve in the French Foreign Legion (the Legion denies that he did, but as he would presumably have enlisted under a pseudonym the denial might not be relevant), he presumably did so during the first decade of the century. By 1909, however, he was a captain in the Indian Army and it seems unlikely that any term of service in the Legion could have lasted very long. He seems not to have been on active service in 1909, and the evidence of his early publications suggests that he was then working as a teacher. His first published work was *The Indian Teacher's Guide to the Theory and Practice of Mental, Moral and Physical Education* (1910), the first of three books which he wrote for Longmans' Practical Indian Education Series. He produced other works in this vein and contributed to scientific textbooks for use in Indian schools.

Wren's first six novels, plus one short story collection, were published between 1913 and 1917, although most of them must have been written some years before publication, because he was actively involved in the Great War for the latter part of that time-period, mostly serving in Africa. There was a consequent hiatus in his publications between 1917 and 1924, punctuated only by the very atypical light-hearted romance *Cupid in Africa* (1920), which does not appear in lists of his published works included in his later novels.

These early novels were not very successful, but the basic patterns which were to recur throughout his work were present from the very beginning. *Father Gregory* (1913) begins with a scene in which an English gentleman is who has been waiting on an Indian railway station for ten days for the woman he loves—wondering all the while whether she might after all have decided to stay with her drunken brute of a husband—is bitten by a rabid dog. He refuses to go in search of medical help lest she arrive and find him gone, but when she does eventually come the sound which greets her as she approaches his tent is "a horrible crowing bark—that was not the barking of a dog." She goes mad, and is still mad when her husband—whose name is William Pooch—comes to reclaim her. She is already pregnant by her lover, and subsequently bears a son, but Pooch callously disposes of the boy and makes every effort to ensure that she will never see him again.

The main part of the narrative of *Father Gregory* is set thirty years later. It seems to be influenced by Joseph Conrad's novels about the redemption of disgraced human wrecks in the far-flung outposts of the empire, especially *An Outcast of the Islands* (1896) and *Lord Jim* (1900). The story follows the exploits of a young man (the mad-woman's son) in the Clubland of the Raj—a setting which features prominently in all Wren's Indian novels—with special reference to his relationship with the saintly priest, Father Gregory. At the end, as the hero meets a noble death after many tribulations, Father Gregory reveals, in a move more reminiscent of Mrs. Henry Wood's *East Lynne*

(1861) than Conrad, that "he" is the unlucky young man's long-lost mother.

This unrepentantly absurd melodrama is rather crudely executed, but is possessed of a curious narrative intensity. That intensity and its attendant emotional power is the driving force of Wren's work, expressed again and again in variations on the same theme. The formula runs as follows: a man who qualifies as a natural aristocrat by virtue of his innate decency is denied his proper place in society by an accident of birth; this primary misfortune is compounded by other cruel—and often freakish—strokes of fate which ultimately force him to cut all his ties with the past and flee to some perilous far frontier; there he faces danger with reckless courage, constantly inspired by some ideal (sometimes incarnate, sometimes not), loyal service which will eventually reconnect him to his true heritage in the end, if only by lending meaning to his final self-sacrifice.

Such was to be the life story of most of Wren's heroes—perhaps all of those he really cared about. Wren the author, in the guise of arbitrary misfortune, assaults these unfortunates with a harshness which sometimes seems close to sadistic malice. The indomitable power of their own virtue—which makes them utterly determined to do the right thing regardless of any cost to themselves—is always turned back on them by evil circumstance. They are forced to live painfully, often in appalling circumstances, but even when they fall among the scum of the earth, they continue to conduct themselves with awesome dignity and probity. The wages of their virtue and courage are usually those traditionally associated with sin; the majority die, and very few of those permitted who are to live enjoy a happy ending. Whatever their fate, however, the manner in which they meet it always provides the final proof of their intrinsic superiority and a vindication of their right to be recognized as true aristocrats.

Other elements of *Father Gregory* were to be repeated too, although less frequently. Females who achieve seemingly-impossible feats of male impersonation are also featured in *Beau Geste* and in Wren's most peculiar foreign legion novel, *Sowing Glory*, which claimed to be the actual memoirs of such a masquerader for which he had only served as editor. The prologue also set a precedent for many other teasing introductions—some harrowing, some merely puzzling—set many years before the climax which would ultimately explain or resolve them. In the world of Wren's fiction unfortunate events invariably cast long dark shadows, which often blight entire lives.

\* \* \* \* \* \* \*

*The Snake and the Sword* (1914) is a heartfelt study of a man whose phobia regarding snakes earns him a reputation for cowardice which he must go to extraordinary extremes to dispel. This too was a theme which was to recur frequently throughout Wren's work, and its constant redeployment suggests that his attitude to cowardice—or to the possibility of being thought cowardly—might itself qualify as a phobia. Like Wren's other early novels, though, *The Snake and the Sword* makes more concessions to the expectations of popular fiction than *Father Gregory*, eventually arriving at a conventionally uplifting ending.

Wren seems to have been trying hard to find an audience, and he dabbled experimentally in various genres, including comedy and—in *Dew and Mildew* (1916)—supernatural fiction. It was in this spirit of experimentation that Wren produced his first foreign legion story, *The Wages of Virtue* (written 1913; published 1916). It was followed soon afterwards by *Stepsons of France* (1917), a collection of anecdotal tales of legion life, some of which featured the same cast of characters. The claim that some of these stories and some of the incidents in the novel were based on actual experience might have begun as a stylistic device, but it was taken seriously by readers, and Wren eventually wrote a number of pieces about life in the legion which were presented as non-fiction, although there is a certain evasiveness about them which might be interpreted as stopping short of any definite and unambiguous claim that the incidents described actually happened *to him*.

The hero of *The Wages of Virtue* has enlisted in the legion as "John Bull," but his real name is Sir Montague Merline. He has re-enlisted several times because he is in hiding from the world at large; some such concealment is necessary because his beloved wife, believing that he was killed while on a military mission in Africa, has married his best friend. John Bull has become the father figure of a small group of good-hearted comrades-in-arms, who are eventually forced by circumstance to desert the legion. Like Moses, he guides them through a long ordeal in the wilderness, bringing them within sight of safety, but dies in his moment of triumph. He never discovers that one of those he has saved is his son, but the boy's mother is able to deduce his true identity from the account her son gives of his adventure.

*The Wages of Virtue* is rather short on plot, bearing rather too close a resemblance to the kind of military memoir which is full of silly nicknames and darkly comic anecdotes, but it does provide a vivid picture of everyday life in the legion. The novel set in train a process by which Wren was single-handedly to create a mythical image of the French Foreign Legion which remains deeply engraved in British folklore to this day. The idea of concealed identity is so vital to Wren's legion stories that it has become the central pillar of the myth. Everyone nowadays understands what is meant by "joining the Legion to forget," and the fact that the phrase features in so many jokes has not prevented a steady trickle of English recruits crossing the channel in hot pursuit of Wren's dream. It is not surprising that when Wren returned to his literary endeavors in the mid-1920s, he set about producing a new legion novel which would make good the deficiencies of *The Wages of Virtue* by providing a more robust storyline. The striking result of this determination, *Beau Geste* (1924), made his fortune and his reputation.

\* \* \* \* \* \* \*

The highly convoluted plot of *Beau Geste* revolves around two mysteries. The first is an introductory tale narrated by a Spahi officer, Henri de Beaujolais, in which he arrives to relieve Fort Zinderneuf in the Sahara desert, only to find that the Arabs who had besieged it have fled and that the walls are manned by legionaries who eventually turn out to be dead. Before he makes this discovery, shots are fired at his column from within the fort and he sends three men to investigate, all of whom disappear without a trace.

This mystery is left unresolved while the main narrative takes up the story of the three Geste brothers, Michael, Digby, and John. They are poor relations of an aristocratic family whose proudest possession is a famous gemstone called the Blue Water, which is being shown to the three brothers and their cousins one night when the lights suddenly go out. When the lights come back on again the gem has disappeared, and—after much anguish and mutual suspicion—Michael disappears, leaving behind a note to say that he is the thief. His brothers immediately conclude that he has gone to join the French Foreign Legion, but they cannot believe that he really is the thief. One by one they follow him, each of them leaving a similar "confession." The reader knows that John is innocent, because he is the narrator, but shares John's total incomprehension regarding the real identity (and motive) of the guilty party.

Having met up again in the legion, the Gestes find themselves under the command of the insane and sadistic Adjutant Lejeune. Digby is eventually reassigned, but Michael and John remain with the unit when it takes charge of the fort at Zinderneuf, where Lejeune eventually assumes control of their fates after his senior officer falls desperately ill. The company's defense of the fort when it comes under siege is successful but very costly, and John is the sole survivor when Digby—the first of the three men sent to investigate by de Beaujolais—arrives to help him give Michael the "Viking's funeral" he always wanted (and fully deserves). It is left to the Spahi to clear up the mystery of who took the gem and—more importantly—why the theft was a act of great nobility rather than the villain's work it first appeared to be.

The title of the book is, of course, a labored and slightly grotesque pun (a trick which Wren was to repeat several more times). The theft turns out to be a *beau geste* committed by the Geste who has been gifted with the nickname "Beau." The argument of the story is that no one is more greatly to be admired than a man whose heroism leads him to do his utmost to persuade others to think him a scoundrel;

this is the final proof of the fact that the Gestes are the true aristocrats, far more worthy of the name than their more richly-endowed cousins. A sceptic might call attention to the fact that Beau Geste's *beau geste* apparently costs several other good men their lives, but the death-toll was partly cancelled out in the two immediate sequels to the novel, *Beau Sabreur* (1926) and *Beau Ideal* (1928). The former is the respectful story of de Beaujolais's glittering career, while the latter continues the adventures of John Geste, which was eventually to be further extended in the picaresque *Spanish Maine* (1935). Wren also cashed in on the huge success of *Beau Geste* by issuing a collection of quasi-anecdotal tales set in the early days of the Geste brothers' recruitment to the legion, *Good Gestes* (1929).

\* \* \* \* \* \* \*

Wren set out to develop a new central character in *Soldiers of Misfortune* (1929), which tells the story of the luckless Otho Bellême, who sacrifices his aristocratic heritage and promising career as a graduate of Oxford to become a vagabond prize-fighter, and eventually— after much procrastination—finds a destiny of sorts in the Legion. His sacrifice is, however, the result of an absurd misunderstanding rather than a calculated noble gesture, and the climax of his career is simply one more prize-fight, as ludicrously overblown as anything in Sylvester Stallone's Rocky movies.

*Soldiers of Misfortune* lacks the melodramatic panache of *Beau Geste*, but—perhaps for that very reason—sounds an odd note of seeming authenticity which tempts one to hypothesize that it might bear more resemblance to Wren's own experiences. It is, however, only one of several Wren novels which are so utterly obsessive as to invite critics to search for possible autobiographical echoes, and there is now no way of knowing which—if any—really do relate to events in the personal history which the author was so careful to hide away. The novel's sequel, *Valiant Dust* (1932), moves back to the tried-and-true formula; Otho and his new comrades are led into the desert by an insane officer embarked on a mad adventure. By an amazing coincidence, this adventure ultimately reinvolves Otho with the girl the joined the Legion to forget, in circumstances which place him on the horns of a very nasty moral dilemma.

In between the two halves of Otho's story, Wren wrote three other books, making further efforts to increase his literary range. One was his fake memoir of a female legionary, but the other two were convoluted murder mysteries: *The Mammon of Righteousness* and *Mysterious Waye* (both published in 1930). In both of these books Wren goes to astonishing extremes of contrivance to set up elaborate *contes cruels* in which innocent men are ruthlessly punished for crimes which they only seem to have committed. In the former case further complications

117

are added by the tangled and hurtful family relationships which bind the main characters together. Neither mystery features a detective and neither is "solved" in any conventional fashion; in each case the explanation of what really happened is offered to the reader as a way of heightening the horrid irony of what has happened.

As with *Soldiers of Misfortune*, one can hardly help wondering whether *The Mammon of Righteousness* contains echoes of real experience—specifically, whether the appalling mother might bear some resemblance to Wren's own. Whether or not it can be reckoned a revealing book, Wren never wrote another like it, and no one would be likely to characterize it as the kind of story calculated to appeal to the "cleanly-minded virile outdoor sot of people." It may have been an experiment in narrative realism whose lack of success persuaded him that he would do better to stick to exotic adventure stories. He was, however, eventually to return—at the very end of his career—to the production of further studies of the phenomenon of guilt, which were every bit as eccentric and equally harsh in their judgments.

*  *  *  *  *  *  *

After *Valiant Dust* Wren created a third hero whose adventures were to sustain him through several volumes: Captain Sir Sinclair Brodie "Sinbad" Dysart, R.N. *Action and Passion* (1933) describes his ill-fated exploits in the navy, while *Sinbad the Soldier* (1935) extends the account of his misfortunes through a period of service in the Guards. In the final volume of the trilogy, *The Fort in the Jungle* (1936), which is even more downbeat than its predecessors, he ends up—surely to no one's surprise—in the Foreign Legion. *The Fort in the Jungle* parades the sharpest of all the pairs of horns with which Wren consistently equipped the moral dilemmas his characters are made to face. The irresistible call of duty compels him to aid and abet the Asian warlord who has tortured and murdered the woman he loved—a woman who had been (like almost all of Wren's heroines) trapped in a dreadful marriage to a sadistic husband.

There is in *Soldiers of Misfortune* and *Valiant Dust* a distinct and rather unpleasant streak of racist xenophobia. Many of Wren's other novels exhibit the kind of casual racism which was common to the whole British genre of "imperialist thrillers," but in that particular novel sequence it is so starkly manifest as almost to qualify as another of his phobias. Interestingly, the Sinbad series deliberately runs counter to this tendency. By the end of volume three Dysart's original identity has been utterly transformed by adversity, and when he made a belated reappearance in *The Disappearance of General Jason* (1940), he was literally unrecognizable, having undergone a metamorphosis into a dark-skinned follower of Islam which was by no means purely superficial.

Several of the other novels Wren wrote in the thirties returned to the Indian settings of his earliest works of fiction. These include a curious ironic fantasy about the frustrating fulfillment of idle wishes, *Beggar's Horses* (1934), and the two-volume action-adventure story *The Man of a Ghost* and *Worth Wile* (both 1937; the US titles were *The Spur of Pride* and *To the Hilt*). Another departure from his normal fare was *Explosion* (1935), a political fantasy which carries a ludicrously mistaken but undoubtedly sincere dedication to "the friends of....the real India of three hundred million unrepresented peasants, whose sole 'political aspirations' are that the peace, the security, the justice and the protection provided by the British Raj may for ever remain to them undisturbed, unweakened and unchanged."

The plot-formula to which Wren returned again and again was replayed twice more in particularly flagrant fashion in the unusually sober *Cardboard Castle* (1938) and *Paper Prison* (1939). The latter is a harrowing study of two star-crossed lovers—the female one is, of course, unhappily married to someone else—who are kept apart long after the obstacle to their union is removed, because each is dutifully determined not to let the other know a terrible secret which they have both found out independently. The former echoes *The Snake and the Sword* in dealing with a crucial flaw of character rooted in psychology, and helped to prepare the grounds for a much more elaborate and much more clinical study in neurosis, *Two Feet from Heaven* (1940).

*Two Feet from Heaven* tells the story of a clergyman cursed with a disturbing dream who eventually seeks help from a psychoanalyst. He is unable to tell the story of events leading up to the traumatic experience which has caused his problem to the doctor, but does relate them to the sanatorium's senior nurse, with whom he falls in love. Their awkwardly burgeoning romance is, however, doomed, because the clergyman thinks that he is only required to confess to the crime he committed—whose consequences are painstakingly laid out in the framing sections of the book—while the nurse takes the view that he cannot consider himself "cured" while he shirks further expiatory self-sacrifice.

In *The Disappearance of General Jason* (1940), Wren reverted to the adventure story format, but he conserved the same bitterly bleak outlook which distinguishes his other late works. As in so many of his novels, a seemingly trivial misunderstanding generates painful and monstrously horrific consequences. The tortuous plot finally sends its hero to seek refuge from the distressing world of civilized men in a leper colony. This was not Wren's last-published book, but *The Uniform of Glory* (1941) is a sentimental comedy as atypical of his work as *Cupid in Africa*, and it may well have been written some years earlier.

* * * * * * *

Whatever P. C. Wren might have desired or believed, an objective observer must surely conclude that there is precious little in his literary work to offer the least crumb of comfort or reassurance to the "cleanly-minded and virile sort" of person who might harbor heroic aspirations. It is probable that no other writer ever subjected his heroes to such appalling privations or brought them to such bleak rewards; even the lucky few who not only survive but actually get to marry the women they love have first to go through hell, and they always seem to end up that vital two feet short of heaven. Whatever his intentions might have been, the message of Wren's work is that the game of honor, courage, and duty is so crooked that it is simply not worth the candle.

Despite the hopeful motto on Wren's bookplate, the merciless logic of his narratives leads inexorably to the conclusion that to err is human and that the penalty for the slightest error is a burden of agony and misery which only death can erase, and for which even the noblest death cannot properly compensate. If it really was the case that he became a bestseller because he appealed to "all that is best in the great heart of the great public," then the great heart of the great public is far sicker, or at least more bitter, than anyone would credit. Nevertheless, Wren did become a bestseller, and it is undeniable that there is something very special about the sense of tragedy which his books contain and convey.

The underlying rhetoric of Wren's fiction is that the chains of events which he maps out so meticulously are awful to behold and almost unbearable to contemplate. What he says, in essence, is that any world which treated people fairly and decently would find a far better use for its heroes than the one in which his are forced to operate.

It seems abundantly clear that Wren desperately wanted to live in some such better world: a world in which no one would ever have to join the Foreign Legion to forget; in which no good woman would ever end up married to a sadistic husband; in which trivial failures of character would not be magnified into life-blighting stigmata; and in which the population of India really might have cause to be unhesitatingly and eternally grateful to the British Raj. Alas, he knew full well that the world in which he did live could not answer his most cherished hopes, and he seems to have desired very ardently to let everyone else know how full and how well he knew it.

It remains a mystery—and probably always will remain a mystery—why P. C. Wren had such an enormous chip on his shoulder. It was so large that none of the military epaulettes he wore could ever displace or conceal it, but it was so well-disguised that none of the many books he wrote ever brought it clearly into focus. There is, however, more than sufficient sincerity and heartfelt emotion in what he wrote to assure us that he was as brave a man while wielding a pen as he ever could have been when wielding a sword.

# XIII.

# RAYMOND CHANDLER

Raymond Chandler's classic essay on "The Simple Art of Murder" (1944) begins as a merciless indictment of the artificiality and absurdity of the traditional murder mystery, and goes on to offer a passionate justification of a very different kind of crime story, whose virtue resides in its acknowledgment of the realities of the modern world of American crime. The description of that world which is issued in the last pages of the essay is too long and too elaborate to quote here, but it will suffice to say that the account constitutes a comprehensive summary of the unintended and unanticipated effects of the Volstead Act, which entered American law in 1919 in spite of President Woodrow Wilson's attempts to veto it.

The Volstead Act ushered in the era of prohibition; and prohibition begat speakeasies; and speakeasies begat bootlegging; and bootlegging joined in unholy matrimony with illegal gambling and brothelkeeping to beget Organized Crime. The logic of the situation was inexorable; the prohibition by law of the third of three activities—whoring, betting, and drinking—in which large numbers of people passionately desired to indulge, no matter what the law might have to say about them, proved to be the straw that broke the camel's overloaded back. It swiftly resulted in the widespread corruption of police forces and the judiciary—corruption which extended from the very bottom to the very top. Never before in the history of humankind had there been such a sellers' market in illegal services. The Volstead Act enabled American criminals to become very rich, fairly powerful, and, to an unfortunate degree, admirable.

Prohibition itself lasted only until December 5, 1933, when the adoption of the XXIst Amendment to the U.S. Constitution invalided the XVIIIth Amendment—but its effects did not. Once organized, crime could not easily be reduced again to chaos; once trust in the legal system had been sabotaged by a cataract of intimidated witnesses, suborned juries, and bribed judges it could not easily be restored. The Underworld to which the Volstead Act gave birth remained the Underworld over which American city life had to be conducted. Criminals never had it so good again as they had in the days of the bootlegger, but the institutional framework of bootlegging adapted to the new regime by transforming itself into the institutional framework of drug-dealing.

It was, as Chandler was later to argue in his essay, this newly-emerged and "not very fragrant world" with which would-be realists of American crime-writing had to deal. This was a mission of representation to which the narrative conventions of the existing tradition— heavily influenced by English detective stories in the genteel tradition of Sherlock Holmes—were woefully inadequate. Nor was realism of representation adequate in itself to create a new genre. In order that such a milieu could be made into a topic for serious literary work, it was necessary to find heroes who might operate in such a world, to represent the seed of a new moral order that might, at least in ideal circumstances, replace the one which had been lost. Thus, the famous concluding passage of Chandler's essay begins: "In everything that can be called art there is a quality of redemption....down these mean streets a man must go who is not himself mean, who is neither tarnished nor afraid. The detective in this kind of story must be such a man. He is the hero, he is everything. He must be a complete man and a common man and yet an unusual man. He must be, to use a rather weathered phrase, a man of honor, by instinct, by inevitability, without thought of it, and certainly without saying it. He must be the best man in his world and a good enough man for any world...."

Because the streets down which he goes are so very mean, it is difficult for this kind of hero to be a policeman, because a policeman—even an Untouchable one who is not himself corrupt—is bound into an institution where corruption is endemic. It is better if he can be a private detective, because his morals, in order to be good, must be entirely his own. But it is not sufficient simply to find a social niche into which an appropriate hero may be fitted; he must also be credited with a distinctive method of dealing with his work and his world. If a hero is to be a force for the redemption of his world, he must be able to move freely within it without ever being absorbed by it. Like all knights errant, he requires a suit of armor which will prevent the slings and arrows of outrageous fortune from lodging in his heart.

The writer of ritualistic fantasies whose pretence of realism is conventionally thin supplies this kind of armor in a straightforward manner, by giving his hero a gun. But a gun is only an "equalizer" when the good are not so very heavily outnumbered by the bad and the ugly; the more recourse a writer has to the awesome magic of the lightning draw, the more fantastic and ritualistic his narrative becomes. In any case, a gun is poor armor against the forces of creeping temptation, and may easily become their ally. Gunmen, like other superheroes, always tend to become outlaws, unable in the end to do much in the way of redeeming society because they do not share the frail flesh of those who live in it. In fantasies which aspire to a more honestly problematic species of realism the power of violence—especially the power to kill—must be acknowledged as a danger to moral health, and its user must be shielded against its recoil. Even if the moral shield is to be reckoned a matter of "instinct" and "inevitability," it must still be delineated with care, and effectively made manifest.

What Raymond Chandler did in the fiction which he wrote to practise what he preached—knowingly and respectfully carrying forward the work of his fellow-crusader Dashiell Hammett—was to define the attitude which befitted the role of the private detective, and to delineate with extraordinary precision the exact balance of cynicism, efficiency, and sentimentality which might be necessary to preserve private virtue in a world where the law had recently regressed from being an ass to being an asshole.

\* \* \* \* \* \* \*

In the same year that the Volstead Act was passed, H. L. Mencken published his book on *The American Language*, which surveyed with a dramatic combination of scholarly scrupulousness and journalistic forthrightness the differences between American English and the domestic variety, and unashamedly celebrated the unique features of the former.

As literary editor of *The Smart Set* ("A Magazine of Cleverness," according to its subtitle), Mencken was enthusiastic to promote distinctively American writing, thus helping to free American literature from the distortions of narrative voices inherited from England, but the magazine was always financially precarious. In 1919, therefore, Mencken and his co-editor George Jean Nathan decided to start a downmarket pulp magazine which might serve as their cash cow. They toyed with the daring idea of aiming a magazine specifically at a black audience, but eventually decided that a crime pulp was a safer bet. In 1920 they launched *The Black Mask*. It served its purpose magnificently, and when its circulation had climbed to a quarter of a million Mencken and Nathan promptly sold it for a hundred thousand dollars (having launched it on a capital of five hundred) and ploughed much of the money into their new brainchild, *The American Mercury*.

Mencken never said a complimentary word about *Black Mask*, and never allowed his name to appear on it, but it was stamped from its inception by his attitudes and interests. Under the aegis of its longest-serving editor, Joseph T. Shaw, it was to preside over the evolution of a new kind of crime story: the "hard-boiled" detective story. Such work turned a coldly unsentimental eye upon the Brave New World of American crime (Woodrow Wilson, perhaps unsurprisingly given the results of his failure to veto the Volstead Act, was rumored to be a *Black Mask* fan), and its writers invented a new way of talking about that world which eventually came to seem uniquely and distinctively American. By a curious twist of irony, though, the Chicago-born man who did the most to develop the new narrative voice had spent his formative years in England, and had been educated at Dulwich College.

The original template for the role of the private detective had been laid down long before the founding of *The Black Mask* by Allan Pinkerton, who founded the Pinkerton Detective Agency in 1850. Like any typical American entrepreneur, Pinkerton had devised an advertising slogan for his organization and had invented one of the most memorable of early logos to go with it: The Eye That Never Sleeps. Pinkerton published books of accounts of his more interesting cases in the days of the dime novels, and others had followed suit, but in the early twenties fictional American detectives were still mostly cast in the amateur-heroic mold of dime novel detective Nick Carter. It was Dashiell Hammett, a former Pinkerton employee, who brought the wind of change into this situation with a series of *Black Mask* stories recounted in the first person by an unnamed employee of the Continental Detective Agency, which culminated in the novel *Red Harvest* (1929).

The Continental Op (as he came to be known in the absence of any other identifier) was not the first private detective to figure prominently in the pages of *Black Mask*. He was preceded by Race Williams, the invention of Carroll John Daly, who embodied many of the characteristics which were to become generic. Williams was disinclined to trust anybody, ever avid to get into a fight, and much given to peppering his dialogue with contemptuously witty remarks. His heart of stone could be melted by a damsel in distress, albeit briefly, but evil and injustice moved him to blazing anger—and what mostly blazed was his gun. He narrated his own adventures, and devoted a good deal of time to explaining to the reader why it made sense to shoot the villains down like dogs instead of handing them over to the due process of the law. Perhaps he protested just a little too much, given that he also devoted a lot of attention to painstaking descriptions of the effects of his fists and his bullets on the bodies upon which they infallibly impacted. Despite his private investigator's license he was not really a professional, and he enjoyed the same mysterious freedom from prosecution that was gifted to most gun-happy amateurs by their creators.

The Continental Op was different because he operated within much narrower limitations of competence and ambition. He was much less fond of shooting and hitting people than Race Williams, and he was sufficiently enthusiastic to avoid being shot or beaten up himself that his everyday behavior was very much less provocative. He didn't brag about the effect of his bullets, and his self-justifications were those of a common mortal trying to do a difficult job rather than those of a fully-licensed avenging angel. He didn't allow himself to be distracted by the temptations of the flesh while he was at work, even though he smoked, drank, and lusted as much as the next man. Perhaps most important of all, he was fully aware of his own inadequacy to do more in the face of everpresent corruption than adjust a very few minor injustices, and he was equally aware of the ironic absurdity of such band-aid tinkering. His recognition of this absurdity was laconic and understated, but it pervaded his narrative accounts of what he did and said.

It is perhaps unfortunate, in retrospect, that Hammett abandoned the Continental Op in order to confront more fantastic heroes with more conventionally-exciting mysteries. Sam Spade in *The Maltese Falcon* (1930) is not so very different a character, but the convoluted mystery which confronts him is entirely artificial—gaudily fanciful, in fact. The hero of *The Glass Key* (1931) is no professional, and he too is faced with a classic puzzle of the kind in which it seems that no one could have committed the murder except the person he wishes to prove innocent. With *The Thin Man* (1932) Hammett deserted *Black Mask* altogether, adopting as his model the kind of gentlemanly "amateur sleuth" who was attaining new heights of popularity in England, thanks to the novels of Agatha Christie. He ran thereafter into an alcohol-assisted writer's block which never let up. Where Dashiell Hammett left off, however, Raymond Chandler soon took over.

\* \* \* \* \* \* \*

Chandler was six years Hammett's senior, and he was forty-five years old when he published his first story, "Blackmailers Don't Shoot" (1933), in *Black Mask*. He had earlier been a businessman in the oil industry, but his career had fallen victim to the effects of the Depression. As an American in England he had always felt like an outsider in his younger days, but because of his long absence and English education he had also felt like an outsider after returning to his own country. In consequence, he was far more aware of the differences between the English and American languages than most, and far more sensitive to the distinctions which those differences represented and cemented. When he began to write in what he saw as a newly-emerged American argot, he felt his way as carefully and as calculatedly as he could, and made rapid progress.

Between 1933 and 1939 Chandler wrote twenty short stories and novelettes for *Black Mask* and its imitative rival *Dime Detective*. The detectives who featured in them wore several different names, where they were named at all, but they were all very similar. They featured as first-person narrators in twelve of the twenty, but Chandler did not settle on that narrative mode without first experimenting with the alternatives. When he eventually began to write novels he did so by "cannibalizing" these shorter works, carefully weaving two or three of them together into plots which became—under the syncretic pressure of this method—unusually convoluted. During this process of rewriting he expanded both the dialogue and the descriptive passages of the shorter works, unifying their perspectives into the single narrative voice of a detective who now acquired the name of Philip Marlowe. This reworking can be tracked in minute detail by comparing the cannibalized stories collected in *Killer in the Rain* (1964) with the three novels derived from them: *The Big Sleep* (1939), *Farewell My Lovely* (1940), and *The Lady in the Lake* (1943). In the novels which he wrote from scratch—the first was *The High Window* (1942)—Chandler maintained the pattern which had emerged from his recombinative work: multi-stranded, intricately-interwoven plots, carried forward by carefully-elaborated descriptive passages and strings of hard-edged dialogue.

The accumulation of "clues" leading to an eventual solution of some central enigma is never an orderly business in Chandler's work. Marlowe's objectives frequently shift in a markedly uneasy fashion, which became steadily more uneasy as his career progressed. Marlowe's critics often point out that in spite of his loyalty and dogged determination, it is relatively rare for him actually to succeed in doing what his clients ask him to do, or for them to get much satisfaction out of it if he does. Indeed, his clients are frequently as corrupt as the world into which they send him to do their bidding, and serving the cause of right while dutifully discharging his responsibility to the payers of his fees sometimes throws up moral dilemmas of a particularly thorny kind. Chandler occasionally played games with his readers in respect of these moral dilemmas, as in the novella "Red Wind" (1938), where the detective's apparent dishonesty is revealed in the last line to be a *beau geste* in disguise.

Unlike most of their *Black Mask* contemporaries and most of those who followed in their footsteps, Chandler's detectives were never much given to solving their problems with guns. Marlowe inherited from his predecessors, and brought to full flower, a world-view which assumed—without ever making a big deal out of it—that bullets didn't really count as solutions at all. Marlowe's armor was not his gun but his point of view, as displayed in the language of his narration and the stylization of his dialogue. For Marlowe, all conversation was a kind of combat in which he tried relentlessly to upstage his adversaries with offbeat wit and canny perception. His first-person narration was an extension of that combat in which—with the reader looking over his shoulder—he engaged the whole sick and sorry world in a one-sided duel of merciless, illusion-penetrating description and evaluation. When he traded witticisms with inarticulate gangsters they usually got nasty, but they were only acting in accordance with the way of the world. In this way, the new reality of the American Underworld provided a whetstone to hone the blade of Chandler's idiosyncratic version of the American language.

In terms of plotting, Marlowe's insistence on talking instead of shooting translated itself into doubt about the clarity of justice. He was unable to go along with the line of argument which Race Williams passed on to Mickey Spillane's trigger-happy Mike Hammer, that although the law had been muddied the ideals of justice had not. Like the

Continental Op, Marlowe took it completely for granted that the evil which was in the world was everywhere, and could not be exorcized—except in the rituals of fantasy—by selecting out those it possessed most powerfully and blowing them away.

Marlowe was never entirely sure where the sword of retribution ought to fall, and he was not given to towering rages of righteousness. In fact, he seemed to invest the greater part of his emotional energy in simply staving off despair. His heart was not hard by any natural inclination, but rather seemed to have become so out of anxiety that if it were once allowed to melt it might simply flow away. In the end, his faith having been progessively shaken and shredded by the sad unravelling of the peculiarly self-motivated inquiries of *The Little Sister* (1949) and *The Long Goodbye* (1954), and unreconstituted by the dour revelations of *Playback* (1958), Marlowe gave in and finally got a girl, but that was the end of his career. Chandler, by then in his seventies, never could complete the novel which looked set to be his *Thin Man* (although Robert Parker has recently done it for him, in an appropriately unsatisfactory manner).

* * * * * * *

Despite the popularity reflected by its awesome sales figures, *The Black Mask* never acquired respectability during its own lifetime. Neither Hammett nor Chandler achieved immediate success when their works were issued in book form, and they acquired their best-selling status by slow degress. That eventual success was, of course, greatly assisted by two celebrated movies which placed Humphrey Bogart in key roles, *The Maltese Falcon* (1941) and *The Big Sleep* (1946), but there was nothing automatic about the process. *The Maltese Falcon* had originally been filmed in 1931 with Ricardo Cortez as Sam Spade, and its plot had already been recycled once, in the Bette Davis vehicle *Satan Met a Lady* (1936), before Bogart finally breathed life into its movements.

The first film adaptation of a Chandler story involved borrowing the plot of *Farewell My Lovely* for a 1942 episode in a series of detective thrillers featuring "The Falcon," a character originally drawn from the work of Michael Arlen. Unfortunately, Arlen was an Armenian-born convert to upper-class Englishness whose works belonged entirely to the highly artificial tradition which Chandler loathed. The plot of *The High Window* was similarly plundered for the British film *Time to Kill* (1942), featuring the imitation-American detective Mike Shayne. Chandler had become active in Hollywood himself, writing the script for the classic Billy Wilder film of James M. Cain's novel *Double Indemnity* (1944), before *Farewell My Lovely* was filmed again, as *Murder My Sweet* (1944), with a woefully unconvincing Dick Powell as Marlowe.

# Raymond Chandler

Chandler's own involvement with the film version of *The Big Sleep* was limited; he was one of three scriptwriters—one of the others was William Faulkner—who between them generated sufficient confusion that no one has ever managed to figure out who killed the luckless chauffeur whose untimely death provides one of the minor details of the intensively-recomplicated plot. The film works well as a film, but could not reproduce the unique qualities of Chandler's writing. A more daring attempt to capture the essence of Marlowe's viewpoint was made in Robert Montgomery's version of *The Lady in the Lake* (1946), in which the director uses the camera as if it were the detective's own eyes, inserting his own face into a few strategically-placed shots involving mirrors. In the end, though, the device is little more than an ingenious eccentricity.

Chandler could write first-rate screenplays—he followed up *Double Indemnity* with *The Blue Dahlia* (1946) and the Hitchcock classic, *Strangers on a Train* (1951)—but this was not at all the same thing as translating his own literary work to the screen. The limitations of the cinema medium and the conventions of contemporary film-making inevitably reduced his robust literary voice to a mere whisper, no matter who took on the task of adaptation. Film dialogue has to be stripped down to the bare essentials in order to fit into the time-scale of a movie, and direct first-person narration has to be stripped down even further if it is to be rendered into voice-over. Chandler's prose is rich in aphoristic remarks, but it is far more complicated than the simple chain of one-liners to which it has to be reduced in movies. The cinematic version of Chandleresque language is no more than an echo of the original.

Echo or not, though, the influence of Chandler's experiments with language on movie dialogue has been enormous. Countless *films noir* tried very hard to reproduce the mannerisms of Marlowesque dialogue and Marlowesque voice-over narration, and succeeded well enough to dignify dozens of cheap B-movies with a style and panache which helps them to remain watchable and enjoyable forty years later. The way of talking which modern patrollers of mean inner-city streets have, in real life as well as in the movies, still owes a considerable debt to Chandler. The real-world role of the private investigator has been demystified to the extent that such fictional characters can nowadays only function as a fantasy *cliché*, necessitating their replacement by rebel cops, but the language of the *Black Mask* hero has been handed down even to tersely-inclined heroes who do most of their talking with a gun. Such lineal descendants of Race Williams as Dirty Harry make as much dramatic impact with their sadistic wordplay as they do with their well-aimed bullets.

What H. L. Mencken—who died in 1956—would have thought about the still-extending legacy of *Black Mask*, which became a legend once its lifetime was over, is difficult to judge. He would probably have preferred to see the American language make progress in a more dignified fashion, and might well have felt a twinge of horror at the revelation that in trying to make a little easy money for a good cause, he had set off a process of linguistic evolution whose progeny out-competed the more delicate hothouse flowers which he nurtured so carefully in "the magazine of cleverness." On one of the few subjects on which they were both ever wont to wax lyrical, however—the object of the Volstead Act—Mencken's most celebrated adage ("No man is genuinely happy, married, who has to drink worse gin than he used to drink when he was single") is surely bettered in every possible sense by the remark which Chandler puts into Philip Marlowe's mouth in *The Long Goodbye*: "Alcohol is like love: the first kiss is magic, the second is intimate, the third is routine. After that you just take the girl's clothes off."

# XIV.

## *NO ORCHIDS FOR MISS BLANDISH*

*No Orchids for Miss Blandish* by James Hadley Chase was first published in 1939. The front cover declared it to be "the toughest novel you ever read," and the publisher's blurb waxed lyrical on the subject of its nastiness:

> This is a tale of a girl kidnapped by ruthless gangsters told with incredible and sustained brutality. That the story will shock and horrify must be faced, but this is an age of realism, and the author is determined to reveal "the big shots," "the tough guys" and "the killers" in their true light. He shows them to be outlaws lacking all human qualities; pitiless monsters delighting in the harshest and bitterest cruelties. Slim Grisson, the chief gangster in the tale, will haunt the mind long after the book has been laid down. He is as fascinating to watch as a black mamba and twice as vicious.

The operative word in this blurb is "told," which may appear to be misplaced but is not. The most significant thing about the book is not that it tells of incredible and sustained brutality (although it does), but that the manner of telling is itself unabashedly and unabatingly brutal. To further emphasize this point the jacket copy added an endorsement of the book's uniqueness by James Whittaker, who opined that "There is an evitable and inexorable quality in this murderous tale to be found only in death itself. The atmosphere is rank poison..."

*No Orchids for Miss Blandish* lived up to its publicity. It sold half a million copies in the next few years, most of them in 1940, during the Blitz. It was shocking enough to cause considerable controversy, and the ensuing *succès de scandale* provoked George Orwell to write an essay for *Horizon*, "Raffles and Miss Blandish" (1944), in which he bitterly lamented what he took to be the story's naked sadism. Orwell declared unequivocally that the novel's appeal was intimately akin to the psychological appeal of Fascism and Totalitarianism. But even Orwell, who loathed the book, was prepared to say that it was "a brilliant piece of writing, with hardly a wasted word or a jarring note anywhere."

Orwell observes in his essay that *No Orchids for Miss Blandish* is a literary curiosity, in that although it is set in the USA, and written in a thoroughly American idiom, its author was an Englishman who had never crossed the Atlantic. The jacket copy likens the work to that of James M. Cain, author of *The Postman Always Rings Twice*, but Orwell judges its antecedents a little more precisely in pointing out that the first part of the plot is borrowed from William Faulkner's *Sanctuary*, and that the style is straight out of the pulp magazines which had for some years been sold off at 3d. in Woolworth's under the label "Yank Mags," having been used as ballast by trans-Atlantic cargo vessels.

\* \* \* \* \* \* \*

There can be no doubt that Chase was thoroughly familiar with *The Black Mask*, the pulp magazine which launched the "hard-boiled" school of American crime writing, and its cruder imitators. In appropriating it for himself, though, he extended the moral pessimism characteristic of that school to a logical limit which no American writer ever approached. Orwell contrasts Chase's characters with E. W. Hornung's cricket-playing gentleman burglar Raffles, but this is a juxtaposition of extremes; the originality of *No Orchids for Miss Blandish* is better revealed by comparing those works which are closest to it in spirit, but which still do not aspire to the same moral anesthesia. Mickey Spillane's tough-minded Mike Hammer is a paragon of fervent righteousness and moral scrupulousness by comparison with Chase's characters, whether they be policemen, detectives, gangsters, or psychopaths.

This kind of extrapolation of borrowed cultural materials is not uncommon. What Chase did to the hard-boiled crime story is precisely what Sergio Leone and other Italian directors did to the Western in the 1960s. He took aboard the milieu and the melodrama, but left out the noble defender of the American Dream who usually features as the hero in native versions of the mythos, substituting characters who are far more morally ambiguous. It is at least arguable that Chase's gangster stories, like the best Spaghetti Westerns, offer a more accurate account of the true essence of their respective genres than the American originals; they accept that what readers actually like about the stories is the violence and the gunplay, not the defense of the American Dream.

According to all the major bibliographical sources, Chase's real name was René Raymond, and he used a contraction of this name (R. Raymond) on one book, *Slipstream: A Royal Air Force Anthology* (1946), which he co-edited with David Lyndon. He also wrote one early novel as James L. Docherty, sixteen as Raymond Marshall, and one as Ambrose Grant, but it was as James Hadley Chase that he remained famous—or perhaps one should rather say notorious.

When he wrote *No Orchids for Miss Blandish* Chase seemed to have found a winning formula, and a measure of success did indeed come his way in later years. *No Orchids for Miss Blandish* was filmed twice, though neither film could begin to do it justice, and the slickest of his early exercises in the James M. Cain vein, *Eve* (1945), was made into an effective film by Joseph Losey in 1965, starring Jeanne Moreau. Complications arose, however, not only because *No Orchids for Miss Blandish* itself proved as shocking as its publicity anticipated, but because it sparked off a remarkable boom in similar stories as beleaguered paperback publishers, struggling to survive in a time of increasing paper shortages, flocked to milk the new-found popularity of such fiction for all it was worth. The resultant orgy of nasty-mindedness provoked local watch committees to embark upon a seven-year moral crusade against gangster fiction, which resulted in many attempts to ban particular titles and subsequent prosecutions for obscenity, some of which were successful.

Chase, inevitably, was a prime target of this moral crusade, and *No Orchids for Miss Blandish* was at one point temporarily withdrawn from sale; his later novel *Miss Callaghan Comes to Grief* (1941) occasioned a prosecution, and he went into voluntary exile. He spent the rest of his life in Switzerland and France. Although he made a far better living thereafter than the other writer notoriously forced to leave the country by the same moral crusade—Stephen Frances, the original "Hank Janson"—Chase's fortunes waned steadily. The kind of critical reputability which Cain and the *Black Mask* writers belatedly achieved in America never came his way.

Even Mickey Spillane has been hailed as a great writer (on account of his uncompromising political ideals) by the recently-deceased darling of the Libertarians, Ayn Rand, but no one—until now—has ever stood up to defend James Hadley Chase against the vitriolic condemnation of his work issued by George Orwell. Nevertheless, the arguments used by Orwell in his attack on *No Orchids for Miss Blandish* cannot really stand up to rational examination, and one could easily argue that if they were valid, they could be applied with equal strength to one of the most famous of Orwell's own works.

\* \* \* \* \* \* \*

The charges which Orwell lays against *No Orchids for Miss Blandish* are straightforward enough. He says:

> It takes for granted the most complete corruption
> and self-seeking as the norm of human behaviour....
> such things as affection, friendship, good nature or

even ordinary politeness simply do not enter. Nor, to
any great extent, does normal sexuality. Ultimately,
only one motive is at work throughout the whole
story: the pursuit of power.

Actually, the main motive at work in the story is the pursuit of
money, but the difference is slight enough not to matter. The point is
that the characters have no scruples whatsoever in pursuing their ends;
even the police have no respect for the law, and take it for granted that
giving prisoners "the third degree" is the most sensible—because it is
the most effective—means of pursuing their ends. The gangsters' ability to frighten people is indeed presented as a kind of glamour which
justifies both self-indulgent cruelty and subsequent gloating. The om-
nipresence of violence is simply taken for granted.

Orwell expresses his puzzlement at the apparent popularity of
the savage violence which plays such a large part in this book and various other contemporary works. He wonders why entrenched soldiers,
who have to face real machine-gun bullets on a day-to-day basis, should
want to while away their time reading about fictitious ones. It seems
ironic to him, if not outrightly paradoxical, that Londoners living
through the Blitz should crave such obviously synthetic "excitement" in
their reading material.

Perhaps it is not so very surprising that men who live in fear of
real bullets and real bombs should take some comfort from reading
about ones which cannot hurt them, but even that excuse may be missing the real point. There is a sense in which the world-view of *No Orchids for Miss Blandish*, in which violence is universal and haphazard,
and must be accepted in all its horror as a simple condition of existence,
must have been far closer to the real everyday experience of Britain's
beleaguered soldiers and blitzed civilians than the morale-boosting
world-view of the newspapers and radio broadcasts which continually
told them what heroes they were for nobly defending the world against
the forces of evil.

The real point at issue, however, is not why the inhabitants of
a world beset by violence of one kind should be interesting in reading
about another kind, but the assumption made by Orwell that in depict-
ing brutal acts and the utterly unscrupulous pursuit of personal advantage, Chase is glorifying those acts and inviting his audience to approve
of that pursuit. This is an assumption which is very frequently made by
members of the literary establishment when looking at works they do
not like, although they never apply it to works which they admire. No
literary critic ever worries about the corrupting influence of the brutality and unscrupulous pursuit of ambition displayed in *Macbeth*, or
wonders about the curious perversity of those who flock to the theatre
to see it.

## No Orchids for Miss Blandish

It is unhesitatingly assumed by everyone that the fact that a man's eyes are plucked out on stage in *King Lear* need not imply that Shakespeare approves of such actions or that he is appealing to the secret nasty-mindedness of the members of his audience. The opposite assumption tends to be made, however—equally unhesitatingly—when the work under consideration is a pulp magazine, or a best-selling novel, or a so-called "video nasty." Ironically enough, it is thanks to George Orwell that we have a word for this sort of tendency; it is a kind of doublethink. It is also a kind of snobbery. The assumption is that cultured men reading great works of literature do so with an appropriate sensitivity, whereas uncultured men reading popular fiction cannot, because they—or the books they are reading, or both—lack the necessary sophistication. (There is a certain propriety, therefore, in the fact that in the last paragraph of "Raffles and Miss Blandish" we find the diehard socialist Orwell reluctantly offering a defense of the value of "snobbishness" as a check upon undesirable behavior.)

In this particular case, though, Orwell wants to do more than simply deride the intellectual capabilities of the sort of people who like the sort of book he thinks *No Orchids for Miss Blandish* is. Having discussed the text, he goes on to argue that the alleged glorification of power and power-lust which, in his view, account for the popularity of the novel is exactly what lies behind the hero-worship of rulers like Hitler, Mussolini, and Stalin. In *No Orchids for Miss Blandish* Orwell therefore finds a symptom of the pattern of historical development which, he feared, would end in the world he depicted in *Nineteen Eighty-Four* (1949)—where, in a very striking and oft-quoted line, the party man O'Brien invites the entrapped Winston Smith to imagine the future as a boot stamping on a human face forever.

So far as I know, no one has ever before suggested that when Orwell wrote that memorable line, he was remembering the plot of *No Orchids for Miss Blandish*, where boots, rubber hoses, truncheons, and lighted cigarettes spend a lot of time inflicting painful indignities on human flesh, but the suggestion may be less outlandish than it seems, and it is a point to which I shall return. For now, it is sufficient to note that Orwell's worst fears about the possible consequences of dictator-worship have been unrealized. Given this, we may perhaps be entitled to wonder whether he might not have made a mistake in estimating the reasons for and evaluating the significance of the huge success of *No Orchids for Miss Blandish*.

\* \* \* \* \* \* \*

The summary of the plot of *No Orchids for Miss Blandish* which Orwell offers in his essay is deficient in one significant respect, in that it grossly misinterprets the ending. The erroneous reading may not be not crucial to his general argument, but the error is nevertheless revealing.

What happens in the story is that the initial kidnappers of the heiress (who is always referred to as "Miss Blandish," never by her Christian name) quickly fall foul of a rival and much nastier gang, who are thus enabled to get away with her without having left any evidential traces of their involvement. The gang's murderous spearhead is the psychopathic Slim Grisson, who hates everyone and everything in the world except his mother (he is strangely akin to the James Cagney character in Raoul Walsh's 1949 film *White Heat*, who might conceivably have been modelled on him). Slim is perversely fascinated by his beautiful victim, although he has previously been unable to relate to women at all. His mother, perceiving an opportunity to assist her son's belated character-development, beats and terrorizes the girl into faking a tiny measure of enthusiasm for his lecherous advances. For this reason alone she is kept alive, while police enquiries get nowhere.

Miss Blandish's desperate father enlists the help of a private detective, Dave Fenner. Unlike the private eyes in *Black Mask*, Fenner is every bit as mean as the streets which he inhabits (although he becomes rather less mean when his own story is continued in the later novel *Twelve Chinks and a Woman*, 1940). In *No Orchids for Miss Blandish* there is no moral distinction at all to be drawn between Fenner and Eddie Schultz, the sanest member of the Grisson gang, who—thanks to a combination of Fenner's enquiries and simple bad luck—ultimately falls into the hands of the police and is tortured until he betrays his friends. At the end, Slim is gunned down and Miss Blandish is freed, but before Fenner can return the luckless girl to her father she commits suicide.

Orwell misrepresents this ending by saying that Miss Blandish kills herself because she has learned to cherish Slim's sexual attentions and feels unable to live without him, although the text says no such thing. Orwell must have been aware of his casual overstatement, because he was sufficiently embarrassed by it to add a defensive footnote to later versions of the essay which says: "Another reading of the final episode is possible. It may merely mean that Miss Blandish is pregnant. But the interpretation I have given...seems more in keeping with the general brutality of the book."

Nowadays, of course, we have become familiar with the syndrome by means of which kidnap victims sometimes do develop strong erotic attractions towards their kidnappers. It is unsurprising, therefore, that we find Orwell's interpretation made explicit in the second film version of the story, Robert Aldrich's *The Grissom Gang* (1971), in which the character of Slim is softened, so that he becomes a good-looking victim of a poor upbringing. Nevertheless, this is not what Chase actually wrote and the text makes it perfectly clear that it is not what he intended.

Chase later wrote a sequel to *No Orchids for Miss Blandish*, *The Flesh of the Orchid* (1948), which reveals that Miss Blandish was indeed pregnant when she defenestrated herself, and that her child grew up to be a psychopathic *femme fatale*, but this belated endorsement of Orwell's alternative reading is not really relevant. The key passage which conclusively demonstrates the wrongness of Orwell's interpretation is not Miss Blandish's final speech—in which she states that she will never be rid of Slim because "I've got him inside me, he wouldn't leave me alone, ever—and now he never will"—but the earlier passage which describes events immediately before Slim is gunned down. In that passage Miss Blandish wishes fervently and quite unequivocally that he will shoot her dead because she feels herself to have been so utterly soiled by his attentions that she can no longer bear to go on living.

This paragraph is, in a sense, a summary of the entire world-view of the story, which is that the utterly and irredeemably corrupt world which it depicts so frankly is one in which decent, happy human life is impossible.

Although he concentrates almost exclusively on the thoughts and actions of other people, there can be no doubt that the central character of Chase's story is the kidnap victim whose defloration and degradation are sarcastically reflected in its title. It is a kind of horror story, and the only thing which prevents that from being obvious is that it is not told from her point of view. But there is a sense in which the most horrific aspect of terrible events cannot be communicated by a fevered account of the emotions of those who are suffering; there are some things so horrible that a narrative tone of cold clinicality is not only adequate but uniquely appropriate to their description.

We can see this kind of muted clinical narration in some of the futuristic novels written in the years immediately preceding 1939, in which writers looked forward to the devastation of cities by fleets of bombers dropping poison gas—two notable examples can be found in the later pages of Joseph J. O'Neill's *Day of Wrath* (1936) and S. Fowler Wright's *Four Days War* (1936). More importantly, we can see it in those descriptions of the worst horrors of World War II which were written afterwards, particularly in descriptions of events in the Nazi death-camps. In such cases as these, the facts speak for themselves with awful clarity; they have no need of an emotionally-charged commentary.

Once we understand this, we can see much more clearly what kind of a book *No Orchids for Miss Blandish* is, and why it was so popular at the time of its publication. At the height of the Blitz, it must have seemed to all clear-sighted people, whether they were cultural sophisticates or not, that England—which surely deserved to be reckoned a Country of the Bland, or at least the bland-ish—was on the brink of Armageddon. As things turned out, Armageddon was averted, and

136

Hitler's much-feared chemical arsenal was never deployed against his external enemies, but it was a damnably close-run thing.

It is perhaps odd and certainly unfortunate that so many people need to be constantly reminded that the aim of horror stories is, after all, to horrify. The purpose of presenting literary images of a world overrun by brutality and populated by psychopaths is not to advocate and applaud such things, but to lament their presence in the real world. It is true that this may be easier to perceive when the mean streets of such a fictional world are trodden by at least one man who is not himself mean, but the absence of such a man is merely an extra dimension of lamentation; it is not a kind of narrative treason. *No Orchids for Miss Blandish* is indeed a shocking book—or was in its day—and in its power to shock lies it strength and its merit.

It was grossly insensitive of George Orwell, and the moral crusaders whose fellow traveller he was, to presume that the world which James Hadley Chase depicted, with its "atmosphere of rank poison," was one of which Chase or his readers approved. In fact, *No Orchids for Miss Blandish* is a tragedy. Its style is not the style of *Macbeth*, although its theme is, but that is not to say that its style was poor, or inappropriate to its time and its audience. The story suggests, but does not hope, that life may be a tale told by an idiot, full of sound and fury but signifying nothing; it is precisely because that is such a horrible suggestion that we all need to be continually reminded of it, just as kings need jesters to whisper continually in their ears the stale news of their own mortality.

The moral of the story told in *No Orchids for Miss Blandish*— and it is an implicit moral, although it has no one to state it—is that a world devoid of heroes, in which the virtuous can only become victims and lose their virtue in being victimized, is a kind of Hell, and that it is a kind of Hell which the real world may be in danger of becoming. George Orwell evidently could not quite perceive this moral in *No Orchids for Miss Blandish*, and thus could not believe that it was the author's intention to deliver such a message. This failure was probably a corollary of his lack of sympathy for the author's method (although we must recall that he thought the book "a brilliant piece of writing").

Perhaps, though—as I have already suggested—George Orwell learned more from reading *No Orchids for Miss Blandish* than he thought. He did, after all, go on to write a novel of his own about a world devoid of heroes, in which the virtuous can only become victims and lose their virtue in being victims. That novel too is about a world which is a kind of Hell, and a kind of Hell which the real world seemed to its author to be in danger of becoming. It was, of course, *Nineteen Eighty-Four*, whose imagined world and narrative conclusion are not only every bit as bleak as the ending of *No Orchids for Miss Blandish*, but are bleak in a remarkably similar fashion. The endings of the two books do differ, though, in one important respect. In *Nineteen Eighty-*

*Four* Winston Smith, unlike Miss Blandish, really does end up loving his persecutor.

No doubt that ending seemed to George Orwell to be "more in keeping with the general brutality of the book."

# XV.

# THE TRIALS OF HANK JANSON

The evolution of the British publishing industry was brought to a virtual standstill by the Second World War and its attendant paper shortages, at what would otherwise have been a period of rapid change. The growth of popular paperback publishing had just begun, and although Penguin was able to obtain a generous quota of paper on the grounds that theirs was a very economical form of publication, most of the other publishers keen to develop paperbacks were held back by the awkward circumstances. A vacuum of demand built up as the war progressed, which small publishers struggled to fill by printing books in very slim formats on paper which was mostly unsuitable for the purpose. When the situation slowly eased during 1946 and 1947, there was a mad entrepreneurial rush to grab a share of the market; the inevitable result was an unprecedentedly fierce competition, which only the fittest could hope to survive.

Most of the new paperback publishers modelled their products on the American paperbacks which—having been far less inhibited in their development by the war—had already become immensely successful. The American paperback companies had inherited their marketing strategies from the pulp magazines, which offered lowbrow fiction categorized by genre, fronted by gaudily seductive covers. The new companies had to discover very rapidly which kinds of fiction would sell best in the UK, and then mass-produce them.

It quickly transpired that the heaviest demand was for two genres: slightly risqué romances and "hard-boiled" American gangster stories imitative of the huge wartime bestseller, *No Orchids for Miss Blandish*. The former usually appeared under French-sounding pseudonyms, the most prolific writer in this vein being "Paul Renin" (Richard Goyne). The latter were mostly signed with American-sounding names, and the biggest success in this line was secured by "Hank Janson," a pseudonym originated by Stephen Frances. Hank Janson's career came to a spectacular climax shortly after Frances had sold the pseudonym to a rival publisher and emigrated to Spain; seven books signed with that name became the subject of a celebrated obscenity trial.

In his book on *The Uses of Literacy* (1957), Richard Hoggart—who was later to be a defense witness in the more celebrated ob-

The Trials of Hank Janson

scenity trial involving *Lady Chatterley's Lover*—laments the postwar boom in these kinds of fiction. In the chapter on "The Newer Mass Art: Sex in Shiny Packets," he lumps risqué romances and gangster novels together as "sex-and-violence novels." His principal objection to such works is not so much to their content as to the mediocrity of their prose style and their formularization. Hoggart's whole book is a bitter jeremiad against what he perceives as an insidious and unfortunate replacement of "authentic" working-class culture by mass-produced entertainments; he sees the standardization of such products as something to be regretted regardless of their actual nature. The fact that the fierce competition favored writers who could write enormous amounts of copy to tight deadlines for miserably low fees was to Hoggart just one more facet of the ongoing disaster, for which no critical allowance could or should be made.

Hoggart's dismissal of the risqué romances—which he calls "Laforgue novels"—is fairly cursory, but he takes a greater interest in the gangster novels, whose ideative origins he finds (possibly having been pointed in the right direction by George Orwell's *Horizon* essay on "Raffles and Miss Blandish") in such semi-respectable novels as William Faulkner's *Sanctuary* (1931) and James M. Cain's *The Postman Always Rings Twice* (1934). Like Orwell before him, Hoggart complains about the "sadism" of gangster novels and the fact that their stories take place "in a world where moral values have become irrelevant," but he similarly pays tribute to the occasional power of the writing, observing that the irrelevance of moral values means that the gangster writer—unlike the Laforgue novelist—cannot shock simply by violating moral expectations, and must therefore by "truly creative," albeit in a limited way, in making descriptions of violence both vivid and disturbing. He observes that the writing "strums on the nerves of the readers," and concedes that some passages are "monstrously effective." In the end, though, he condemns the books for their combination of fatalism and nihilism, believing that the absence of the kind of "larger pattern" which contains and develops out of the action of *Sanctuary* is a fatal flaw:

> We are in and of this world of the fierce alley-way-assault, the stale disordered bed, the closed killer-car, the riverside warehouse knifing. We thrill to those in themselves; there is no way out, nothing else; there is no horizon and no sky. The world, consciousness, man's ends, are this—this constricted and overheated horror.

Hoggart continues to labor this point. He reiterates the claim that real Literature is not like this, and that the nihilism of gangster fiction must be deemed a kind of "narrowness" or an "immaturity."

140

Having thus condemned the undeniable power of this kind of fiction as something tainted by failure, he then feels free not to ask any more questions about why the fiction was so powerful, and why it was so very popular in some circles and so very unpopular in others that the vengeful wrath of the law was visited so furiously upon it.

* * * * * * *

    Stephen Holland's recent book on *The Trials of Hank Janson* (1991) offers a meticulous account of the court cases which took place in 1953 and 1954, involving seven Hank Janson books which were charged with being obscene.  Certain phases of the account seem faintly surreal and rather farcical.  Gerald Dodson, the recorder in the first trial (which involved the publishers but not the author), found it very tiresome that the defense wanted the jury actually to read the books before passing judgment on them.  He observed that he had "glanced through" the books himself, and had been able to reach the conclusion that they were obscene "with no difficulty at all."  He eventually conceded that the jury might be allowed to read the books before reaching a verdict, but added:  "I am loath to inflict the task upon them; it seems a ghastly way of spending their time."  Given that the fifty-odd Hank Janson titles issued between 1948 and 1953 had probably accumulated total sales in excess of four million copies, it seems odd that the learned gentleman should find it inconceivable that anyone could want to read one, and one can only wonder what a dreadful sense of shame must have descended upon any jury-member who actually had read one.

    The appeal court, headed by the Lord Chief Justice, Lord Goddard, later decided that Mr. Dodson's conduct of the trial had been impeccable and that his remarks could not possibly be deemed prejudicial.  The Lord Chief Justice added that having had the "misfortune" to read the books involved, he could not see that anyone could have come to any conclusion but that the books were "grossly and bestially obscene" and "filthy."  He opined that if they were read by adolescents it was no wonder that there was so much juvenile crime.

    Both Dodson and the appeal judges flatly rejected the defense case, which was that the general standards of acceptability in contemporary literature were such that the publishers had no reason at all to think that these particular books contained anything uniquely objectionable. They declared that filth was filth and always would be, and that if other books contained similar material, they too were ripe for prosecution. Indeed, one of the appeal judges, Mr. Justice Gerrard, stated flatly that it was "high time that publication of this stuff was stopped."  He so effectively declared open season for the prosecution of publishers that the ensuing glut of obscenity trials eventually caused parliament to modify the law.  The new Obscene Publications Act, modelled on a draft prepared in 1955, eventually became law in 1959; it permitted exemption from prosecution on the grounds of literary merit, and paved the way for the publication of *Lady Chatterley's Lover*.

After the failure of their appeal, the publishers of Hank Janson were sent to jail, and Stephen Frances returned from Spain in order to stand trial himself. This trial collapsed, however, after Frances claimed that the seven books in question were actually the work of his successor. An examination of the accounts of the publisher revealed receipts made out to one Geoffrey Pardoe, which appeared to be payments for some of the relevant books, so the prosecution was abandoned. No attempt was made to prosecute Pardoe in Frances's stead, and no one seems to have queried the fact that the receipts produced in court were for absurdly small amounts (£20 for one book, £125 for a batch of half a dozen). Given that the Janson books in question had print runs of 100,000, these figures seem woefully inadequate to qualify as payment. Holland speculates that Frances might have been able to deny having written the books because he had in fact dictated them on to tape, and that the fees paid to Pardoe might have been for supplying plot ideas (or, perhaps, simply for transcribing the tapes).

The seven books named in the original trial were *Accused*, *Killer*, *Pursuit*, *Vengeance*, *Amok*, *Auctioned*, and *Persian Pride*. The first five were part of the fourth series of Janson gangster novels, each series having comprised twelve books. (The fifth series was aborted after the second volume in consequence of the conviction, although the pseudonym was sold to another publisher and was soon revived, continuing in regular use for many years.) The other two were "specials"—a label given to Janson works in other genres; in this case exotic romances of slavery set in the Middle East.

In the early series books "Hank Janson" had been the central character and narrator of all the stories, having purportedly been a sometime soldier of fortune and longtime crime reporter for a Chicago newspaper, but only two of the five series titles involved in the trial—*Killer* and *Vengeance*—feature the Hank Janson character, even though the other three also take the form of first-person narratives.

Modern readers would have considerable difficulty in detecting the faintest hint of what is nowadays thought of as "obscenity" in any of the seven books. Despite what the various judges said about the irrelevance of changing standards, it is now possible to describe in minute detail in any kind of fiction acts which Hank Janson would have been constrained to refer to in extraordinarily oblique terms. The books are, indeed, just as intimately concerned with sex as they are with crime, but they approach this subject in an extraordinarily roundabout fashion, which continually involves their author in ambitiously suggestive (but conscientiously inexplicit) beating around the bush.

*Accused* is a drastically-simplified imitation of *The Postman Always Rings Twice*. A young drifter is on the run because of his involvement in a hit-and-run accident, the other people in the car (who were really responsible for it) having attributed the blame entirely to him. He is taken on as hired help by an exploitative roadhouse proprietor who keeps his wife as a literal slave and uses her sadistically. The drifter is attracted to the wife, and when caught *in flagrante delicto* with her is forced to kill her husband in self-defense. As they flee together the woman treads on broken glass, and the wound becomes infected; the youth dares not take her to a hospital but obtains some morphine tablets with a stolen prescription, on which she overdoses. All this is told in a series of flashbacks while the youth is being tortured by the police, who deem him guilty of three brutal murders and are enthusiastic to extract a confession. At the end of the book, as the jury at his trial retires to consider its verdict, he screams at its members: "Please don't find me a killer. Please don't make a killer of me!"

*Pursuit* is the story of a robbery which goes wrong. The grimly laconic tale is told by an ex-convict who has been going straight for some years for the sake of his wife; it begins when the wife has just died of a heart-attack while in police custody, having been mistakenly accused of shop-lifting. The narrator is invited to resume his safe-cracking career by his one-time partner in crime, but the venture is doomed from the start by the inadequacies of the various others involved, who include an ambitious but overconfident young gangster, a brutal driver with a nymphomaniac wife, and a cynical "inside man" who ultimately fails to resist the temptations of the nymphomaniac. The two old pros fail to escape after the others have made an irredeemable mess of things, because the narrator's friend is futilely carrying a torch for the cocky gangster's girlfriend, who is similarly damned by her own love for the gangster.

*Amok* begins in a condemned cell, where the narrator is sweating away the hours before his execution. He was a crooked lawyer, who began carrying a gun when a disgruntled client sent assassins after him, but shot the wrong man by mistake. He fakes a suicide attempt in order to get into the prison hospital, from which he escapes with another prisoner who managed to supply him with a gun. The two of them go on the run with the narrator's loyal girlfriend, who has helped to set up the break-out. The other prisoner is an out-and-out psychopath who commits several casual murders, terrorizes and imprisons the narrator, kidnaps a young woman in order to rape her, and ultimately rapes the narrator's girlfriend. The narrator eventually kills him, but is badly wounded in the process. The ending is rather neat. While the escape was becoming gradually more nightmarish, the narrator wondered whether he might wake up in the condemned cell to find that it has all been a dream, and in the last chapter he does indeed wake up in exactly the same situation; the reader is compelled to follow him through a long reprise of chapter one before the author confirms that all the horrors have, in fact, been real and that this is his second time around.

# The Trials of Hank Janson

*Killer* and *Vengeance* are noticeably less effective than than these three criminal-as-victim stories, largely because they must labor under the handicap of having a hero. This is a handicap not so much because nothing excessive can happen to the indestructible Hank, but because heroes do not really belong in this kind of story at all. In both books Hank figures as an action-man detective of sorts, dodging bullets and frustrating robberies, but such matters are mere routine, and are handled in a rather desultory fashion. The true central character of *Killer* is a gold-digging nice-girl-gone-wrong who is determined to use her sex-appeal as a way out of poverty, while the true central character of *Vengeance* is an embittered reporter, dehumanized by the five years imprisonment he has served for a crime he did not commit, who sets out to take his revenge on the witnesses who testified against him, and very nearly ends up getting framed all over again. In a way, their stories might be more interesting if Hank were not in them, partly because Hank assiduously saves them from the worst consequences of their actions, and partly because his constant moralizing about the way misfortune and society have corrupted two potentially nice people belabors a point made much more succinctly by the books which have no objective commentator, and which therefore allow events to speak for themselves.

Hank does, however, have another function within the books in which he stars, and that is to experience at great and tortuous length the pangs of lust. Hank is very vulnerable to female charms, but he is the perpetual victim of his own high moral standards. He is constantly being vamped by assorted prostitutes, nymphomaniacs, and teasing gold-diggers "practising" their wiles, but he is forced by his contempt for their insincerity to battle desperately—and not always successfully—against the awful force of his own sexuality. He is much given to uttering quaint little homilies while this sort of thing is happening about the virtual helplessness of mere men in the face of assertive female sexuality.

Hank, being a very manly man, prefers to do the chasing and the pressuring himself, although he likes a girl who will flirt with him a bit, and play the seduction game as it is meant to be played. He tends to let really nice girls alone, figuring that they deserve someone steadier by far than he, but he is perpetually disappointed by the fact that such relationships as he does form always go wrong. One reason for this, of course, is that the series nature of the books means that any alliance he forms can only be temporary, but long-term fans could not help but notice that since the early days of *This Woman Is Death* Hank had grown progressively less able to form even temporary liaisons. The real purpose of this apparent ill luck is to add to the pitch of frustration which he reaches when tempted by the kind of girls he does not want.

The covers of the series novels—which seem to have been a major factor in persuading judges that one hardly needed to read the books to know that they were obscene—are an apt visual synopsis of Hank's view of womankind. They all show large-eyed, heavily-made-up, big-breasted women in strapless evening gowns assuming more-or-less provocative poses, and one can easily tell that these are not the kind of girls that any sensible man would want to get seriously involved with. Any doubt that might have remained on this score was frequently dispelled by the titles affixed to volumes in other series: *Lola Brought Her Wreath*; *Women Hate Till Death*; *Skirts Bring Me Sorrow*; *Silken Menace*; *Nyloned Avenger*. During earlier moral panics some of these covers had been oversprayed with silver paint, and a few had been omitted in favor of inoffensive silhouettes of Hank himself. It was by no means unknown for books in this period to be charged with obscenity on the basis of their covers alone, despite the fact that bare nipples and skimpy underwear were strictly taboo; the almost-full-frontal female nude on the cover of *Flame of Desire* by "André Latour"—which was promptly banned—was a rare and striking exception.

The strained and highly ambivalent attitude to sex which is the definitive feature of Hank's admittedly rather one-dimensional character is also a key feature of the crime novels in which he does not appear. The safecracker in *Pursuit* successfully resists the nymphomaniac, but not without difficulty, and it is the failure of his compatriots to discipline their lusts as successfully as he which damns them all. The loving sexual relationships which the murderers in *Accused* and *Amok* form—against all the odds—are unceremoniously devastated by the relentless pressure of the plot, and turned into litanies of anguish.

The tortuousness of these relationships actually contrasts quite sharply with the perfectly straightforward torture which the female protagonist of *Auctioned* undergoes when she is sold into slavery after the massacre of her nomadic tribe. When she rejects the advances of the loathsome Caliph whose agent buys her, she is imprisoned and whipped, and her systematic degradation then becomes an unlikely stratagem in a battle of wills between her owner and a dashingly handsome political rival who finds her extremely attractive.

*Auctioned*—and *Persian Pride* and *Desert Fury*, which continue and conclude the story—really are mild and fairly orthodox pornography, in the eccentric tradition of the Victorian classic of naughtiness, *The Lustful Turk*. Its references to genitalia are far from explicit, and it is the threat of rape rather than its actuality that moves the plot, but the whipping scene is straightforward textual voyeurism (significantly, *Auctioned* is not a first-person narrative). The world of the series novels is not much like Chicago, but it is very much the milieu of the contemporary *film noir* which is their real inspiration, and it has a comfortable gloss of second-hand realism; the world of *Auctioned* and its sequels is a fatuous fantasy. Any slight plausibility obtained by means of its obvious borrowings from P. C. Wren's *Valiant Dust* and E. M. Hull's *The Sheik* are painfully undermined by limitations of style.  The Caliph is called Syd, his chief wife is named Dallas, and such dialogue as there is tends to the unintentionally hilarious ("You have spoken to thy Mother, beloved."/"Thou and me are intended for each other").  These are books which are trying as hard as they dare to be naughty, but in doing so they serve to illuminate by contrast the fact that the series novels are doing something very different.

The run-of-the-wordmill Janson titles make every effort to draw out as vividly as possible the scenes in which Hank or some other poor sap is jerked around by his avid glands, sadly and desperately aware of the fact that said glands are perfect suckers for artifice and outright dishonesty and will only lead him into trouble.  The novels carefully compare and counterbalance this kind of internal beating with external beatings of all kinds.  Their subject matter is pain, physical and emotional, and their essential, relentless message is the inescapability of such pain.  Unlike *Auctioned*, they are not diluted masturbation fantasies; they are blackly humorous lamentations of the absurd existential situation which opposes the internal forces encouraging masturbation with external forces which strive to repress, deny, or redirect their internal counterparts by determinedly and stupidly pretending that they are something other than they are.

This is an issue about which both Stephen Frances and Geoffrey Pardoe seem to have harbored strong and sincere feelings.  Frances had been brought up in poverty, and fancied himself an ardent sympathizer with the plight of all victims of social injustice and hypocrisy; he was ardent enough, at any rate, to have joined the Communist Party and subsequently got himself expelled for his outspokenness.  Pardoe appears to have had a more privileged upbringing, but one of the few books to which he attached his own name is *This Is a Mystery*, a book published in hardcover in a "private edition" by Frances, which is a condemnation of social attitudes to sexuality, and the harmful consequences of repression and ignorance.  *This Is a Mystery* includes a curious diatribe against "wantons" which is a plain-speaking version of the attitude to loose women so graphically displayed in Hank's heroic tussles with miscellaneous vamps and tramps.  Whichever man wrote the books involved in the trial, there is every reason to suppose that he took their underlying world-view seriously.  The opposition which Hank the author and Hank the character offer to the judges and cops and prison warders and psychopaths who embody and represent the inescapable and life-denying oppressions and repressions of "the world" is real enough, and the books' depictions of the tragic perversity of whores, gold-diggers, and nymphomaniacs—no matter how ludicrous the portrayals of such women may be in literal terms—are by no means impotent as metaphors.

* * * * * * *

The Lord Chief Justice of the day seems to have believed that books like Hank Janson's, which frequently use criminals as narrators, might encourage impressionable readers to commit crimes. Actually, any reader who felt in the least encouraged by the hopeless image of criminality presented in these books would be worse than a fool. Lord Goddard also seems to have believed that attributing eager sexuality to women, and alleging that males could be thrown into a state of tortured anxiety by their own lusts, was "grossly and bestially obscene." Some people might suspect, however, that this was a classic case of a milord protesting just a little too much.

It is really irrelevant whether or not one chooses to admit the rough-hewn likes of Hank Janson to the elevated world of "Literature," or to the vulgar realm of popular culture, or whether one insists on treating them as something else entirely. Perhaps the passage of time will one day allow critics to be as generous to Hank Janson as they nowadays are to the *films noirs* that were his inspiration, and which have been so ennobled by their French soubriquet that the term "B-movie" has almost become a compliment. In any case, it needs to be observed that what Richard Hoggart thought was their failure—the "narrowness" which prevented them from being truly literary—is really part of their essence. It is precisely their tight focus, the sheer relentlessness of their nihilism, which generates a special kind of sympathetic bond between reader and character.

Even at its blackest, the *film noir* preserved a steadfastly polite respect for the officially-approved mythology of sexual attraction; in 1953, Hank Janson must have seemed to many of his readers the only man in the world who had taken it upon himself to share with ordinary blokes like them the deep, dark secret which we all shelter in our innermost hearts: the knowledge that the official mythology of sexual attraction is just as full of what Hank politely insisted on calling "baloney" as the officially-approved myths of the nobility of judges, the impartiality of the criminal justice system, the sanctity of the nuclear family, and the spontaneous good fellowship of Christmas. Perhaps that was the principal reason why respectable folk thought he was so dangerous.

# INDEX

Barrie, J. M., 15
BBC, 92
*Beatrice* (H. Rider Haggard), 25
*Beau Geste* (P. C. Wren), 5, 112-120
*Beau Ideal* (P. C. Wren), 117
*Beau Sabreur* (P. C. Wren), 117
*Beggar's Horses* (P. C. Wren), 119
Bell, Neil, 52
*Ben-Hur* (Lew Wallace), 96
*Benita* (H. Rider Haggard), 25
Benoît, Pierre, 26
Benson, E. F., 87
Benson, Edward, Archbishop, 87
Bentley, George, 77, 79-80
Besant, Walter, 68
bestsellers, *passim*
*The Big Sleep* (Raymond Chandler), 126
*The Big Sleep* (film : 1946), 127-128
"The Black Cat" (Edgar Allan Poe), 89
*The Black Mask* (magazine), 123-128, 131-132, 135
"Blackmailers Don't Shoot" (Raymond Chandler), 125
Blake, William, 80
Blavatsky, H. P., Madame, 64
*The Blue Dahlia* (film), 128
*The Blue Lagoon* (H. de Vere Stacpoole), 12, 14-17
body-swapping in literature, 67-74
Boer Rebellion (1881), 21, 24
Boers, 20-21
Bogart, Humphrey, 127
*Book of Nonsense* (Edward Lear), 32
Bowdler, Thomas, 33, 62
Bowman, Isa, 33
Boyer, Charles, 90
*The Brass Bottle* (F. Anstey : novel), 72
*The Brass Bottle* (F. Anstey : play), 72
Bristol, England, 70
*British Birds* (W. H. Hudson), 38
British Empire, 22, 49, 60, 95
British Foreign Office, 20
*British Weekly* (magazine), 47
Brummell, Beau, 58
Buddhism, 47
Buenos Aires, Argentina, 38

Bulwer, Henry, uncle of Edward, 20
Bulwer-Lytton, Edward, Baron Lytton of Knebworth, 7, 20, 57-66, 95-96, 103-104
Burroughs, Edgar Rice, 16, 45
Burton, Robert, 70
*Bye-Ways* (Robert Hichens), 88
*Byzance* (Jean Lombard), 64
Cagney, James, 135
Cain, James M., 127, 131-132, 140, 142
Caligula, Roman Emperor, 93
Calpurnia, Roman mistress of Emperor Claudius, 98
Cambridge University, 47, 58, 69
Campbell, Thomas, 60
Capra, Frank, 47, 53
*Cardboard Castle* (P. C. Wren), 119
Carib Indians, 13
Caribbean Islands, 81
Carroll, Lewis, 29-37
Carter, Nicholas, house pseud., 124
Cartland, Barbara, 86
*Catherine Herself* (James Hilton), 47
*The Cave Girl* (Edgar Rice Burroughs), 16
Cerridwen (Celtic goddess), 98
Cetewayo, King of the Zulus, 21
*Cetewayo and His White Neighbours* (H. Rider Haggard), 21
*Chains* (Henri Barbusse)—SEE: *Les Enchainements*
Chaka, Zulu King, 27
Chandler, Raymond, 121-129
*Les Chants du Maldoror* (Lautréamont), 103
"The Charmer of Snakes" (Robert Hichens), 88
Charterhouse, 99
Chase, James Hadley, 5-6, 130-139
Chicago, Illinois, 123, 145
*The Child of Ocean* (Ronald Ross), 15
*Children of the Morning* (W. L. George), 17
"The Chimes" (Charles Dickens), 70
Chopin, Frédéric, 48

149